CURTAINS AND BLINDS

EILEEN KITTIER

WARD LOCK

First published in Great Britain in 1986
by Ward Lock Limited, Artillery House, Artillery Row,
London SW1P 1RT, a Cassell Company.

First paperback edition 1990.

Designed by Niki fforde
Drawings by John Castle
Text filmset in Bodoni
by Tradespools Ltd, Frome, Somerset

Printed and bound in Spain by
Graficas Reunidas

ISBN 0–7063–6851–7

ACKNOWLEDGMENTS

The author and publishers would like
to thank the following for kindly
providing photographs for the book:
Harrison Drape page 31
Osborne & Little plc pages 11, 49, 53
Sanderson page 71
Swish pages 14, 25
Sunway Blinds pages 35, 63, 69, 77
Syndication International Ltd pages 21, 55

CONTENTS

INTRODUCTION

Many people remark that they do not know where to begin when it comes to making curtains. They are presented with so many choices. Which fabric and what colour? Which track or pole and where to position it? What style of curtains and heading, and how much fabric will be needed?

The answers to these questions depend partly on your budget, and partly on your requirements as curtains have many purposes: insulation, shade from sunlight, privacy, aesthetic appeal, and on occasions to obscure an unwelcome view.

Windows are essential to let in light and air, but unfortunately they also let out vital heat. Lined and interlined curtains help to overcome the problem of heat loss, and exlude draughts. Interlined curtains, as the name suggests, have a layer of thick, soft, fluffy fabric between the outer curtain and the lining. The thicker and more dense the curtains, the less draughts will be able to penetrate, and any air that is trapped between the layers will act as insulation. Where circumstances permit, it is possible to use several window treatments at one window; a blind in the reveal, and a pair of curtains on the wall outside the reveal. There are many thermal linings available and although they are more expensive they will eventually pay for themselves by savings on heating. Another way of cutting down on draughts is to take the curtains beyond the sides of the window, then take the outer edges of the curtain back to the wall when the track projects into the room. Floor-length curtains certainly give a warm feel to a room, but it is not advisable to fit them over radiators, thereby cutting out heat and possibly damaging the fabric as well.

Sunlight is always welcome, but it can make a south-facing room very warm in summer and it can fade fabric and shorten the life of curtains. Light-coloured linings will reflect a certain amount of sunlight and give some protection to curtain fabric, but they can cut out too much light if the curtains are drawn during daylight. Louvre drapes (vertical slatted fabric blinds) or Venetian blinds, which are making a come-back, are a better solution. They are marvellous at deflecting the sunlight while still allowing a certain amount of light into a room, and at the same time they protect inner curtains.

The need for privacy will depend upon the situation of your home. If it is in a secluded position you may feel there is no need for further privacy. Side-dress curtains that are not operational could be used for appearance with perhaps a sheer, which would soften the window, particularly at night. However, in built-up areas where houses are more likely to be overlooked you may wish to cover your windows during daytime without losing too much light. One of the following suggestions may solve the problem: a roller blind of transparent fabric; a café curtain which covers the lower half of the window permanently, leaving the top half uncovered; a Venetian blind; louvre drapes, or a sheer. Alternatively, use curtains with a heading fixed in a closed position across the window opening, and draw the curtains away from the middle of the window, tying them back to let in just enough light to suit your purpose.

Although many people consider window treatments as functional, there are others who regard them as an important decorative feature and derive great pleasure from their appearance. They not only soften the hard outline of the windows, but also contribute to the ambience of a room by way of their colour, texture and style.

Part I provides the background information, on interior design and basic curtain-making techniques, to help you decide on your requirements. Parts II and III give step-by-step instructions on how to make different types of curtains and blinds, from simple unlined curtains to the more complex swags and tails.

Currently we are enjoying an exciting revival of some of the more elaborate and 'romantic' window treatments of the past, such as festoon blinds, pelmets, valances and swags and tails. We also have a tremendous variety of fabrics to suit every conceivable décor, purpose, design and price range. The combination of these styles with beautiful fabrics, together with the constant stream of ideas from advertising and the media, should enable us to express some of the creativity that is within us by being a little more adventurous with our window treatments.

PART I

1 INTERIOR DECORATION

COLOURS, TEXTURES AND PATTERNS

Curtains and blinds can form a focal point in a room, and should not only harmonize with the overall interior décor but also enhance it. The success of your scheme will ultimately depend on the harmony and proportion of your colours and furnishings in relation to the size of your room.

Style and colour are a matter of personal taste. Colours, textures and patterns affect everyone differently so there are no hard and fast rules, but there are some guidelines that will help you with your choice.

Colour can affect mood and create atmosphere. Blues and greens, for example, are considered to be cool and restful; yellow is thought of as sunny and gay; while red, orange and tans are associated with warmth, as are peach and apricot.

At the outset, think about the type of feeling you want to create in the room—whether formal or informal, restful, lively, elegant or cottagey. The room itself may suggest a character, particularly if it is in an old period house. The main colour in your scheme should reflect this mood. Restrict this colour to large areas such as walls, carpet or curtaining and build up from here, introducing one or two further colours or tones of one shade, and adding interest with patterns and texture.

Texture affects colour. A colour will seem brighter on a smooth, hard surface and more muted and darker on a rough, softer surface. Texture provides contrast in a room, and adds further interest and another dimension.

Patterns can be fun and some people are very adept at mixing them successfully. If you are uncertain about a particular balance, keep to plain colours and introduce just one pattern into the room. Alternatively, use co-ordinated patterns which have been designed to blend together. Bear in mind that large patterns are eye-catching and can be very dominant. And if too many patterns are used together, they will detract attention from each other, thus losing impact. A beautiful design is worth making into a feature, so take care that the overall effect is not too fussy and muddled. When mixing prints, make sure that they have colours in common, or tone well together. The size of a pattern is important, too, particularly in relation to where it is to be used. A large-patterned fabric may be very successful for a full-length pair of curtains but totally overpowering on a short pair at a small window.

Finally, before deciding on a style for your window, stand back and take another look at its size in relation to the rest of the room. Decide whether the room would benefit by altering the proportions of the window, which can easily be achieved by clever positioning of the curtain track. A window can be made to appear larger by fixing the track above the window reveal, at ceiling height if necessary, and extending it beyond the sides of the window. This will give the curtains a larger expanse and create a striking splash of colour. In a small room, however, this could make the room appear even smaller. It is a question of whether the size of the room can take the increased proportions.

CHOOSING A STYLE FOR YOUR WINDOW

Having decided upon the type of atmosphere you want to create with colour, texture and patterns, and having considered proportions, you are now ready to choose a style for your window. Remember that your window is quite likely to be unique.

First consider the alternatives open to you. Conventional curtains are just one option. These can be short or long and with one of several headings. Floor-length curtains, generally, will add sophistication and, with a crisp, hand pinch pleated heading, will suit a formal background. Pencil pleats or a frilled, gathered heading on short-length curtains blend well with an informal, more relaxed atmosphere. Decorative trimmings can be added to emphasize a particular feeling. Braids following the outline of curtains give a formal, traditional appearance. Contrasting binding on the leading edges of curtains (those that come to the centre) will give a sharp definition and a smart finish.

Frills suggest informality and would complement curtains with a channelled, gathered or pencil pleat heading and look most appropriate in a pretty, feminine bedroom or a cottagey kitchen/breakfast room. A frill with the edges bound in a contrasting or toning colour adds a further individual touch, making the curtains a little more special. Café curtains, which traditionally only cover the lower half of the window, offer a very simple solution to privacy and are ideal in kitchens which face onto a busy road. They can be teamed up with an additional pair of short curtains hanging above them which would be drawn at night, thus giving a tiered effect. They can be made even more attractive by the addition of frills or a scalloped heading.

Your choice of curtain track or pole should also complement your style, from an elegant brass pole for a traditional setting to a more modern, unobtrusive track. Pelmets and valances can further emphasize a particular style, as well as hiding any unsightly tracks. The defined outline of a hard pelmet suits formal surroundings whereas a frilled valance will soften the overall appearance of windows, particularly when teamed with curtains that have frilled leading edges. A hard pelmet can be softened, if necessary, by adding a flowing shape such as a scallop to its lower edge.

For a touch of real extravagance, a swag and tail would give a rich and sumptuous finish to curtains in an elegant, formal setting.

Curtains that are draped back and held in position with tie bands can give a completely different appearance to those that hang down straight. They can be held back with stiffened, shaped bands, strips of fabric or ribbons, or with thick, coloured cords with tassels. Another alternative is to drape fabric back over specially designed hold-back hooks in brass or chrome. The higher up the curtains are tied back, the more light you will admit, but by fixing the tie band lower down you obtain a fuller drape in the fabric.

In some cases a blind may be more appropriate, used either on its own or combined with curtains. Roller blinds offer a good deal of scope through colour and fabric combinations, from floral patterns to bold geometric prints. An individual finishing touch can come from your choice of shaped hemline, which could be angular, castellated or scalloped. These blinds are particularly practical in kitchens and bathrooms, being easy to clean.

Venetian blinds are often thought of as being suitable for kitchens but the atmosphere here is inevitably hot and sticky and the slats quickly become grimy. They are then very tedious to clean. Venetian blinds are better suited to a study or workroom where a simple, practical treatment is needed, and where they can be easily dusted over. Their most important asset is the way in which they can deflect light.

Where a tailored, modern and unfussy line is required Roman blinds would be ideal. When these are pulled up they form into defined horizontal pleats which lie on top of each other to look like a soft, layered pelmet.

In complete contrast, ruched or festoon blinds are both pretty and feminine, and can be lavish and opulent, depending on the fabric used and their surroundings. The fabric of ruched blinds is permanently gathered up in rows along its length, forming a ruffled scalloped appearance over the whole surface of the blind. When the blind is drawn up the scallops become even fuller. A festoon blind, on the other hand, hangs like a curtain when it is down but it has vertical rows of rings on the back through which cord is threaded. As it is drawn up, swags appear between the rows of rings, forming a scalloped hemline. These blinds give a beautiful soft line to a window and the scalloped hemline can be further enhanced with a frill.

2 WINDOW SHAPES

It is not possible to describe a suitable treatment for every type of window and there is no such thing as a standard window, since two identical windows located in a different position on a wall may need quite a different treatment. I will, therefore, concentrate on a few problem shapes and situations.

The first point to consider with any window is light. By dressing a narrow window with curtains inside the reveal you will cut out light during the day as there is no additional space in which they can be stacked back. This also applies to festoon, ruched and Roman blinds when fitted inside the window reveal. It is advisable in these circumstances, and in other such situations where light is particularly important, to fit your curtains outside the reveal and extend the track beyond the sides to allow for this stack back, and in the case of blinds to fit the batten above the reveal. The wider the curtains, or longer the blind, the more space needed to accommodate them. In the case of a small pair of curtains, a minimum of 15 cm (6 in) each side should be allowed, increasing progressively with the size of the curtains.

The strategic placing of the track or pole is the solution to many of the problems surrounding window-dressing.

Tall narrow windows can be made into a feature by keeping the treatment simple and fitting a roller or Roman blind within the window embrasure in order to preserve its outline. This type of window would not be suitable for a festoon or ruched blind, however, unless there was enough width for a minimum of two scallops. Alternatively, it would have to be fitted outside the window reveal.

To change the window's shape, you can create width by extending the curtain fixture beyond the sides of the window and placing it as close as possible to the architrave at the top of the window. Fabrics with horizontal patterns will also give the impression of width, and curtains that are draped back will help to break the vertical line that would otherwise be formed by curtains which hang straight down at the sides. A pelmet or valance would also help to reduce height provided it is fixed as close as possible to the top of the architrave, thereby covering the top part of the glass.

Multiple windows are marvellous for creating a bright and airy room but the effect could become over-fussy if the windows are treated individually, particularly if they are of different sizes. The windows can be unified by placing just one track above all the windows on one wall, giving the illusion of one large window when the curtains are closed. During daylight hours the curtains could be arranged either drawn back to either side of the track, or covering the walls between the windows.

In a room where there are windows on diffcrent walls, aim to fix the curtain fitments at the same height to create a unified appearance.

A single corner window presents the problem of where to allow the curtain to hang during daylight. The obvious answer is to draw it back to the side away from the corner, but this can create an unbalanced appearance. An attractive arrangement where light permits is to have one curtain with a heading fixed in a closed position and tie the curtain fairly tightly in the centre of the window with bows. Another alternative would be to fit a blind within the window reveal.

Where there is a window on either side of a corner, again the aim is to unify them. The choice would be whether to draw one pair of curtains to stack back on the walls beside the windows, thus exposing the corner, or to have two separate pairs of curtains that draw from the centre of each window and thereby cover the corner area with fabric. This may cut out a certain amount of light, but as there are two windows in one corner, the room has light coming in from two directions and is probably lighter than average anyway.

A shallow and wide window is not the best proportioned, and is often placed high on a wall. Privacy may not be a consideration, in which case the simplest treatment may be a sheer to soften the window outline; or, for a more cosy feeling at night, combine it with a roller blind. If you want to improve the window's proportions, use a café curtain and place the curtain rod just above the sill level, allowing the curtain fabric (which should be opaque) to cover the wall below to a suitable level. (The window must be above eye-level so that the sill is not visible.) The curtain will create the illusion of a deeper window. You could add a smaller top tier of curtains which could be drawn at night should you want complete privacy.

Windows that pivot from a central point are frequently fitted in modern flats for ease of cleaning. The fitments will need to be placed well above and beyond the sides of the window to give maximum freedom of movement. Sheers would present a problem at this type of window unless they are fixed onto the top and bottom of the pivoting window-frame on rods or wire.

Dormer windows, fitted into alcoves in the roof, are difficult to treat because there is little or no space into which the curtains can be drawn back. Most blinds other than a roller blind will screen out too much light. One straightforward solution for sash windows is to allow minimum fullness in the curtains themselves and tie them back tightly during daytime. A small, shallow valance approximately 15 cm (6 in) deep, with more fullness than the curtains, would enhance the window's appearance and would make very little difference to the light in the room.

Another alternative would be to have cross-over sheers, which present a soft, pretty appearance. On inward-opening casement windows attach sheers, fitted at the top and bottom on wire, and draw in the centre of each curtain with ribbon tied into bows.

Bay windows present the same problem as corner windows: where do the curtains hang during daylight hours? One pair of curtains drawn back to the two outer corners of the bay will look attractive, but they will cut down the light from the side windows. One solution for a large bay is to make one large pair of curtains to fit across the front window and allow it to be free standing, that is, do not fix its outer edges to the corners. Make another pair of curtains, one for each side window. During the day, position the large pair at the middle of the main window and draw in the centre of each curtain with tie bands to form two attractive drapes. Tie the side curtains back to the walls adjacent to the side windows.

Bay windows also lend themselves to blinds of all types. Ruched or festoons could add style to the setting. Roman blinds would suit a squarish bay and could be teamed with a pair of full-length draw curtains fitted across the flat wall in front of the bay, or with dress curtains standing at the sides of the bay.

Bow windows are a natural asset to any room and should be highlighted. They are not difficult to deal with, thanks to the many tracks on the market which can be bent to fit the shape. Floor-length curtains which hug the curve present a beautiful flow of fabric, and can be drawn back to the sides of the window to expose the sweeping curve during the daytime. A valance following the outline of the windows can offer another pleasing effect. If there is a window seat, curtains should hang to sill level. Or a pair of full-length curtains could be hung from a pole across the wall in front of the bow, framing

the windows by day and closing off the alcove at night.

Arched windows are one of the most elegant forms of window, and any treatment which hides the beauty of the classical shape seems like sacrilege. They do pose difficulties in dressing, however, and in some instances there is no alternative but to hang draw curtains from a track or rod placed above the arch.

Shaped curtains fitted to arched windows cannot be operational. The heading must be fixed to the arch, and the curtains are draped back and held open with tie bands. This treatment gives a lovely shape both day and night. It is also possible to use festoon or ruched blinds at this type of window, but they would only draw up satisfactorily as far as the level at the bottom of the arch. For a very simple treatment, dress only the rectangular section below the arch, leaving the top uncovered.

Doors that swing inwards present the problem of curtain fabric interfering with the operation of the doors. One of the most practical treatments with a glass-panelled door, but not necessarily the most attractive, is to anchor sheer fabric to the top and bottom of the glass panel. A roller-blind covering the glass area is an alternative. However, both these methods would be greatly improved by adding full-length curtains at the sides where space allows. These could be hung from a decorative pole, perhaps set well above and extending beyond the sides of the door, to enable the curtains to be drawn well back.

3   FABRICS

SELECTING FABRICS

The choice of a suitable fabric can be daunting because there is such a wide variety of fabrics on the market today. The different combinations of colour, beautiful

designs, textures, fibres and weaves all add up to a vast range of fabrics from which to choose and at enormously varying prices. Ultimately, however, the fabric you select

For this unusual pelmet the design of the fabric has been cleverly used in creating the geometric pattern. The curtains hang very straight to emphasize the striped pattern of the material and give the window a square outline.

for your window treatment should not only complement your chosen style with its visual appearance but it must also suit its purpose. It would be inappropriate to pick a cotton repp, for example, which is a thick, firm fabric for a feminine style with frills. This style requires a soft flowing material such as a lightweight cotton seersucker. Conversely a loosely woven fabric would not be successful for a Roman blind, which requires a firm, stable fabric.

Apart from the visual appearance of curtain fabric, and suitability for its purpose, the other important characteristic to consider is its drapability. Soft, weighty fabrics tend to fall easily into gentle folds; an obvious example is cotton velvet which is both soft, supple and heavy. Every fabric handles differently, and the only way to find out how it is likely to drape when made up into curtains is to hold up a large sample and study how it hangs.

It is always advisable to buy furnishing fabrics rather than dress materials as they come in wider widths and are usually of a more suitable weight. Widths vary from 120 cm (48 in), 130 cm (51 in), 137 cm (54 in), 140 cm (55 in) and 150 cm (59 in). Make a note of the width of your chosen fabric as you will need this information when you come to estimate the amount of fabric needed.

TYPES OF FIBRE

In order to recognize the different characteristics of individual fabrics it is helpful to know a little about the raw materials used (i.e., fibre content) and the weave and various finishes which may be applied to it, as it is the combination of these factors that affect its appearance, how it handles and its performance. Time spent examining and handling fabric for yourself is time well spent as there is no substitute for experience.

Yarns are made from either natural or man-made fibres, and the quality of fabric will ultimately depend upon the type of raw materials used and how the yarn was manufactured into cloth.

Natural fibres are derived from vegetable or animal sources and provide cotton, linen, silk and wool.

Cotton is strong, hard-wearing, easy to handle and relatively inexpensive. It is prone to shrinking and should be pre-shrunk during the manufacture to make it a good buy. It creases easily in its natural form but often has a crease-resistant finish applied to it.

Linen is one of the oldest fibres known and is even stronger than cotton, but it creases badly unless treated with the appropriate finish. It has the advantage of staying clean longer than most other fabrics. Its main use in furnishing fabrics is as linen union, a hard-wearing fabric. Although curtains are sometimes made up in this fabric it is not always satisfactory as it can be rather stiff.

Wool is warm and soft. It has good insulating qualities, and is used in furnishing fabrics mixed with other fibres.

Silk, although it is considered a delicate fabric, is in fact very strong, but it is adversely affected by sunlight. Silk curtains should therefore be lined to give some protection. Some silk fabrics will drape beautifully while others have a light, crisp appearance.

Man-made fibres were first developed to imitate natural ones, and ultimately to keep pace with the growing demand for fabrics, as it is not possible to produce enough from natural sources alone. Many new qualities were introduced into these man-made fibres that could not be obtained from their natural counterparts. Many of the best fabrics are made by using a combination of man-made and natural fibres.

Man-made fibres can be split into two groups, those that are derived from natural sources but have been transformed by chemical treatment, and those that are made totally from chemical sources and are therefore synthetic.

The first group consists of rayon and acetate.

Rayon is frequently blended with other fibres and used extensively in furnishing fabrics. It is soft, and handles and drapes well.

Acetate fibres are blended with other fibres to produce silk-like fabrics that are soft, drape well, and have a rich, lustrous appearance. Many dupions, brocades and moirés have a high acetate content, and all are suitable for curtains. Too much heat during ironing will damage fibres and they should never be damped down during ironing otherwise the fabric will be permanently spoilt with a watermark.

Among the synthetic fibres used in furnishing fabrics are nylon, polyester and acrylic.

Nylon made a great impact on the textile industry when it was first discovered. Fabrics produced from this fibre are fine, strong and hard-wearing can be washed frequently without the shape and size altering, and can be drip dried. They requires very little ironing and an iron that is too hot will melt the fabric. Nylon is crease-resistant and is often mixed with other fibres to give them this quality plus extra strength. One disadvantage, however, is that it acquires static electricity, causing it to pick up dirt easily. Nylon is damaged by sunlight so is not the best fabric to use for curtains.

Polyester has become one of the most successful of the man-made fibres. It is hard-wearing, crease-resistant, easy to wash and quick drying. It is frequently mixed with other fibres, particularly cotton, to impart improved life and easy-care qualities. It is suitable for curtaining as it is not harmed by sunlight.

Acrylic fibres are made into fabric which is soft and warm, and consequently has similar characteristics to wool. It is most commonly woven into textured or pile fabrics and it has an advantage over wool in that when washed correctly (without too much heat) it will retain its shape, drip dry and need little ironing. It drapes beautifully and is consequently most suitable for curtains, with the added advantage that it is not affected by sunlight. It can be blended with other fibres too. Loosely-woven textured varieties are often made up into a heavier type of unlined sheer curtain.

Modyacrylic fibres have many of the same qualities as acrylic. In addition, they are flame-resistant, making them most suitable for furnishing fabrics.

TYPES OF FABRIC

It is impossible to list all the fabrics that would be suitable for window treatments, as the range is constantly growing. Fabrics are not always given a particular name but are often referred to just by the fibre content, e.g., cotton or polyester print. The table describes the standard types of fabric.

Bolton twill A firm, hard-wearing fabric. Should be lined to reduce light penetration.

Brocade A heavy fabric with patterns woven in a jacquard weave. Produced in a variety of yarns. Drapes well.

Buckram A loosely-woven plain weave, impregnated with glue to stiffen. Used for pelmets and in a finer quality for curtain headings. It is not washable.

Bump A fluffy, blanket type fabric, made of plain weave and used as a curtain interlining and to soften pelmets.

Casement A closely-woven plain weave fabric. Drapes well. Usually produced in plain colours.

Chintz A finely-woven stiffish cloth with a glazed finish. Usually printed with highly coloured patterns. If the glaze is produced chemically it will be permanent, otherwise it is liable to wash out.

Cretonne A finely-woven plain fabric. Often printed with patterns with a shadowy outline.

Damask Similar to brocade but traditionally of one colour. Contrasting tones are achieved by a woven matt pattern on a satin-weave background.

In this large, awkward bay window the curtains have been attractively arranged to break up the window but still let in plenty of light.

Domette A fine, plain-weave type of flannelette, with a soft fluffy surface. Used as interlining. It is made of cotton alone or mixed with wool.

Dupion A plain weave, often with a slub surface and with a satin backing. Made mainly of man-made fibres such as viscose, acetate or blends.

Folkweave A loosely-woven cotton fabric, using coarse yarn, often with stripes. It has a rustic appearance.

Gingham A lightweight fabric woven with coloured yarns in stripes or checks.

Moiré A finish applied to the fabric to give it a watermarked appearance. It is used on cotton, silk and man-made fabrics.

Plush A fabric with a long pile, often made of wool or synthetic yarns in the pile and with a cotton ground.

Repp A firm fabric with a heavy weft thread forming a ribbed surface, usually made of cotton, or cotton and wool mixture.

Sateen A strong lightweight satin weave used for linings, and as curtaining with an added print. Mainly made of cotton with a shiny surface on one side where the weft threads lie on the surface.

Taffeta A crisp, plain-weave fabric with a sheen and a slight rib running across it. Fairly stiff.

Tapestry Only fine qualities are suitable for curtains. A woven fabric with an embroidered appearance made of cotton or wool, or mixtures.

Velvet A closely-woven fabric with a short-cut pile on one side. Made in numerous yarns, silk being the most luxurious and expensive. Cotton velvet makes excellent curtains.

LININGS

Lining provides essential protection for the main curtain fabric against exposure to sunlight, dust and dirt.

Cotton sateen is the most widely used lining fabric as it is strong and drapes well, and its shiny outer surface helps to resist dust. It is manufactured in various qualities and widths. It can be bought undyed, bleached or dyed in a variety of colours. Black or dark-coloured linings help to reduce the light penetration into a room but should only be used with an appropriately coloured outer fabric in order not to spoil the appearance of the curtains.

Plain-weave polyester and cotton fabrics are also used as linings. Although the latter may be slightly cheaper than sateen, it may not have the same draping quality.

Thermal linings with a soft, fluffy coating on the inside provide excellent insulation although some do have a rather unattractive rubber-like appearance on the outside. One type of insulating lining has a coating of aluminium on the reverse side which not only provides protection from heat loss in winter but also prevents excessive heat build-up in a room during summer by deflecting the sun's rays. It is also more dense than a normal lining and is thus able to cut out more light.

AFTERCARE

Fabrics are expensive, but they will last for years and give great pleasure provided they are looked after in the proper manner. If large curtains are vacuumed in situ with a hand attachment, this will keep the fabric fresh and prevent a build-up of dust, reducing the need for frequent cleaning. Ruched and festoon blinds will benefit from this attention, as they tend to be dust traps.

Check the care label on the bale of fabric when you are buying it. It is important that the instructions are followed carefully in view of the many different types of fibres and finishes used in modern fabrics. Ask for advice if no cleaning instructions are available.

Curtains that have linings sewn in will require dry cleaning in order to reduce the risk of lining and curtain fabric shrinking at different rates.

Any curtains with stiffened buckram headings should be dry cleaned.

4   CURTAIN HARDWARE

Curtain hardware has come a long way since the days of the narrow brass rod and rings. There is now a large range of fixtures and fittings from which to choose. It is of paramount importance that you select a type that will take the weight of your curtains; after all, the main purpose of tracks and poles is to act as a means of support. You will also want to choose a type that will suit your special needs, for example, you may require it to bend round a bay, and you will need to consider whether a pre-corded version is necessary. (Corded fitments enable curtains to be drawn without handling or soiling the fabric.) In addition you will need to decide whether you want a type that will act as a further embellishment of your scheme or one that blends insignificantly into the background in order not to detract attention from the curtains themselves. Finally, remember when buying your curtain fixture to allow extra length to enable your curtains to be drawn back beyond the sides of the window, where possible.

TRACKS AND POLES

Tracks are made from either plastic, aluminium, steel or brass, and in general those made of metal are stronger. They can be coated with a white, gold, silver or brass finish, either plain or decorative. Some can be fitted with finials, most can be fitted into the wall or ceiling and are usually bought complete with all the necessary fixtures and fittings. A selection is shown in fig. 1.

There are several plastic tracks available, varying in strength, which are suitable for straight runs and which can also be bent successfully round bays. Some have gliders which slot into grooves on the back of the track. Others have all-in-one hook gliders which clip onto the face of the track and eliminate the use of separate curtain hooks. These hook gliders also have a small hole in their

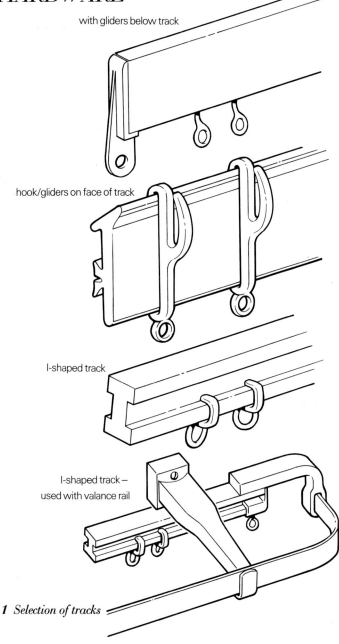

with gliders below track

hook/gliders on face of track

I-shaped track

I-shaped track – used with valance rail

1 Selection of tracks

base which is positioned below the track from which a separate lining can be hung. Optional cording sets with overlap arm are available which enable the curtains to overlap at the centre when closed. However, these sets are mainly for use on straight runs.

Tracks which are cut to measure are essential for the more awkward fitting situations. These strong steel tracks can be cut to length by a supplier, pre-bent to fit an awkward bay, and have the additional advantage of being ready corded.

Steel telescopic or extendible tracks are a good investment because of their adaptable length, making fitting easier, but they are suitable only for straight runs.

The conventional 'I' shaped track made of brass with wheeled runners and rings is now also available in a lightweight plastic version. The former is more suitable for use with heavyweight curtains, but the latter will operate more silently. These tracks can be fitted round bays with the optional use of a cording set, and can be fitted with a valance rail.

Although tracks are now less unsightly, you may still feel they need to be covered with a pelmet or valance. A decorative pole could be the alternative; there is a tremendous range from which to choose, but they are all only suitable for straight runs.

Wooden poles suit an informal, unsophisticated atmosphere, and the untreated type could be painted or stained to suit your décor. They are generally made of a hardwood called ramin with a natural, mahogany or walnut finish, and are available in lengths up to 300 cm (10 ft) with diameters of 25, 30 and 35 mm (1 in, 1⅛ in, 1⅜ in). They are generally supplied with deep projecting wall brackets, up to 88 mm (3½ in), which makes them ideal for placing over radiators or projecting window sills. However, with some varieties it is possible to buy short-reach brackets or recess brackets, if preferred. On wide spans it is essential to use enough support brackets to prevent the pole from bending under the weight of the curtains.

The traditional brass pole will add a touch of classical elegance to a room. These are available in all manner of finishes from bright brass to antique gold and antique brass. The choice of finials ranges from sculptured pineapples and lanterns to simple ball-ends.

Some are manufactured from steel and give the illusion of the classical style but have simulated half-rings that run smoothly on nylon gliders in the back of the pole. These tracks are also extendible and can be purchased in two diameters, 25 mm (1 in) and 35 mm (1⅜ in) and span up to 609 cm (20 ft) although some of the narrower types only span up to 381 cm (12 ft 6 in). In addition they are internally corded with the bonus of an overlap facility.

Narrow rods are intended for use with café curtains and can be purchased with rings and special clasps which simply grip the top of the curtain, eliminating the use of curtain hooks.

Slim-line tension rods, which are telescopic, are used to carry net curtains neatly without any fixing brackets, but they can only be used within a window reveal as they spring out to grip the sides.

ACCESSORIES

There are many useful accessories available which will give curtains a professional finish. They include brackets which enable two separate tracks to be used together (or a pole and a track) giving good clearance between the two sets of curtains. Extension brackets project the track out to avoid protruding window sills and radiators. Recess brackets enable a pole to be used within a window reveal and replace end finials.

Cording sets incorporating overlap arms are available to fit certain straight tracks as an optional extra. An alternative to a cording set is a draw rod, which is a simpler and cheaper method of operating curtains without handling them. It is a slim wooden rod which slips into the first ring of each curtain on the leading edge and, when not being used, hangs out of sight.

Fabric and corded tie bands need to be attached to hooks, and these are available in a range of designs. Curtains can also be elegantly draped back over specially designed curtain-holders.

Essential technical hardware used in making up curtains includes a variety of curtain hooks of varying strengths, made of plastic or metal, which can be sewn on, slotted into pockets on special tapes, or pinned into hand headings.

Weights will improve the hang of curtains. They can be bought either as small, round discs, which are sewn into the corners of curtain hems, or in strip form, to be inserted along the whole length of the hemline. This is sold by the metre in three weights—light, medium and heavyweight.

INSTALLATION

Whatever hardware you choose, it is essential that it is securely fixed, and it is worth thinking about the actual fixing point at your initial planning stage. There are several options open to you (fig. 2): 1. window frame; 2. ceiling of window reveal; 3. wall just above window; 4. higher on wall above the window; 5. ceiling.

Fixing into wood is the easiest method, therefore fitting to the window frame should not present any problem provided the depth of the frame is deep enough to take the track brackets. Make pilot holes, then insert screws.

Positions 2 and 3 could be the most difficult if there is a concrete lintel above the window, as this will involve drilling into concrete. In this instance, it may be easier to fit a batten into the actual concrete, which will require fewer holes. The track or pole could then be screwed into the batten.

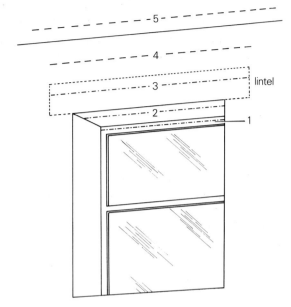

2 Fixing points

Higher above the window there may be brickwork, in which case a batten may again be the easiest method to use. Its only disadvantage is that it will project the curtain fixture further into the room and when the curtains are open the batten will be visible. The resulting space from the end of the track or pole back to the wall is known as the 'return' and can look rather unattractive unless covered with fabric. Attach a screw-eye into the end of the batten near to the wall into which the end curtain hook can be slotted.

When fixing into the ceiling, you should ensure that you screw directly into the joists. If these are not in the right position for your track, you can make fixings with special plasterboard plugs, but you should then avoid hanging heavy curtains.

In modern timber-frame houses, it is possible that you

could be fixing into the timber frame itself and/or plasterboard above the window reveal. In this case, screws fixed into the timber will be quite satisfactory, but plasterboard plugs (cavity fix) should be used in between.

Finally, tracks and poles will benefit from regular attention as dust and dirt will impair their performance. Some tracks are treated with silicone to ensure smooth running, so an occasional polish with a silicone-based spray will help to keep them in good operational order.

5 EQUIPMENT

Prior to making any curtains or blinds, make sure you are properly equipped. There is nothing more irritating than to start a job, and find halfway through that you do not have a vital piece of equipment.

Your most important piece of equipment will be a *sewing-machine*, and you should of course know exactly how it works. Ensure, too, that you always have a selection of spare needles ranging from fine to heavy (70–100). You should change your needle regularly, and not only when it is blunt or broken. Different fabrics require different thread and size of needle. Always practise on a sample of fabric first to find the right combination. One of the most common reasons for a machine not stitching correctly is using a blunt needle or an incorrect size of needle for the fabric and thread.

A large pair of *cutting scissors* are essential. They should be kept in a sharp condition, otherwise they will be no use at all. Bent-handled shears are best of all, as the blades rest flat on the cutting surface.

A *small pair of scissors*, about 15 cm (6 in) long are useful for trimming or unpicking. Embroidery scissors are excellent for this as they have pointed blades.

A *seam ripper* is useful, but should be used with caution to avoid cutting fabric.

Pinking shears are not essential but can be useful. They cut a zig-zag edge to prevent fraying. Never use these scissors to cut paper as this will blunt them.

An *iron*, preferably a steam one, will be needed. The base of the iron should be kept clean. A pressing cloth prevents fabrics from becoming shiny.

A well-padded *ironing-board* is necessary, but when ironing big curtains, a large flat surface is more suitable, softened with several layers of cloth.

A metal *tape-measure* of a good length is essential for measuring your window. A good quality tape-measure that will not stretch is necessary for general sewing use. It should have both metric and imperial markings.

A *padded weight* is useful, approximately 15 cm (6 in) square by 5 cm (2 in) deep, to hold fabric firmly in position and prevent it slipping. To make one, fill a cardboard box with sand or other heavy material. Seal the box with tape, then pad and cover it, attaching a handle across the top.

Tailor's chalk is needed for marking the fabric.

Pins Sharp dressmaker's or glass-headed pins are best. Never use rusty pins as they will mark the fabric.

Have a selection of hand-sewing *needles* to hand, in assorted sizes (1 coarsest–10 finest).

Thread Cotton thread is available in different deniers: 50 for lightweight fabric, and 40 for medium to heavyweight. Synthetic thread is very strong and should be used with synthetic or stretch fabric as it has more elasticity. It is essential to use the correct thread to obtain perfect stitching.

6 HEADING STYLES

The style of heading should enhance the fabric and complement the décor of the room. With the easy-to-use tapes that are available, decorative headings need not present any difficulties to the inexperienced needle-woman. A pencil pleat tape, which produces a deep, stiffened upright heading, will create an overall gathered effect below it. Pinch and cartridge pleats, however, form distinct folds in the curtain fabric below the heading, enabling the fabric to drape beautifully. For the more experienced needlewoman, hand-pleated deep headings can give the great satisfaction of creating beautiful curtains with a professional finish.

It is important to decide on the heading style before estimating and buying the fabric, as the heading will determine (i) how much fullness is needed in the curtains, and (ii) the necessary *heading allowance*, that is the amount of fabric needed to make up the heading. The *heading allowance* should be added to the finished length measurement.

TAPED HEADINGS

Most deep tapes have two or three rows of pockets, making them adjustable for use with all types of track or pole. The top row is used with a pole, or slotted onto combined hook/gliders to prevent the heading from standing well above the track. The lower rows are used with conventional gliders (which hang below the track) so that the heading will cover the face of the track. The deepest headings, approx. 14 cm (5½ in), are used with particularly long curtains to give a better proportion and are sold in two varieties—one for use with a track, the other with a pole.

When applying any tape, always position the free ends of the draw cords, which are used to pull up the heading, to the outside edge of the curtain (i.e., the edge furthest away from the centre). After pulling up the curtain to the desired width, tie the cords neatly but do not cut them off. The heading can then be released for cleaning at a later date.

Standard gathered heading tape

This tape is approximately 2.5 cm (1 in) wide and is available in several colours. A new type is on the market which will produce small groups of narrow pleats in addition to a standard gather, simply by pulling up an alternative set of cords. By placing the tape 2.5 cm (1 in) below the top of the curtains a good-sized frill will form when the tape is drawn up. This heading is generally used with a track. The depth of the frill can be increased in order to conceal a track by positioning the tape further away from the top of the curtain. However, deep frills tend to become floppy and fall forward unless they are slightly stiffened. This tape will achieve a satisfactory curtain fullness with a minimum of one and a half times the track length using a thick fabric, but double fullness is preferable, particularly with lightweight fabrics.

A heading allowance of 4 cm (1½ in) should be added to your finished length to make a 2.5 cm (1 in) frill.

(To apply this tape, see pages 39–40).

Pencil pleat tape

This deep tape is available in several depths, 6 cm, 7.5 cm and 14 cm (2¾ in, 3 in and 5½ in), to suit all sizes of curtains. It needs fabric fullness of two and a quarter to two and a half times the track length, depending on the thickness of the fabric. The thinner the fabric the more fullness is required. It will need a heading allowance of only 1.5 cm (½ in).

A channelled heading with frill above. The curtains drape well and are drawn back to create a pretty outline.

Pinch pleat tape

This tape produces tall, elegantly fanned pleats, with flat spaces between them, by drawing up cords. It is a quick and easy method of achieving triple pleats. It is available in three depths to suit all lengths of curtain. Generally, it requires fabric fullness of exactly twice the track length, depending on the variety. It needs the same heading allowance as pencil pleat tape—1.5 cm (½ in).

The tape should be applied so that the pleats and spaces are symmetrical on both curtains of a pair. It is not a gathered heading. The size of the pleats and spaces are predetermined and cannot be altered. In certain instances, the length of your particular track may not coincide with a balanced pleating arrangement because of the pre-determined size of the pleats, thereby leaving a larger than usual space at one side of your curtain. However, this can be overcome by stitching a small pleat by hand to improve the balance.

Apply this tape as for pencil pleat, bearing in mind the manufacturer's instructions.

Cartridge pleat tape

This tape produces full rounded pleats with well balanced spaces between them. It is 9 cm (3½ in) deep and needs fabric fullness of twice the length of the curtain fixture. The heading allowance is only 1.5 cm (½ in). These pleats are also of a predetermined size and therefore any adjustment is limited, as with pinch pleat tape. It should be treated in the same way as pinch pleat tape. The roundness of the pleat is improved by filling it with a little wadding or a tube of curtain buckram.

FRILLED CHANNELLED HEADING

This is the simplest form of heading to achieve without the use of a tape. The frill is obtained by sewing a channel through a double thickness of fabric below the top of the curtain. Through this a rod, pole or wire can be inserted. The fabric fullness is then gathered along the curtain fixture, creating a frill above it. As mentioned in Chapter 1 this type of curtain heading is fixed and cannot be opened, but the fabric can be draped back and held with tie bands. It is most suitable for lightweight curtains, nets and café curtains, and requires a fullness of twice the length of the curtain fixture, but this is adjustable. Less fullness is needed with thicker fabrics. The depth of the frill is also variable, as with a taped frilled heading. A heading allowance of 7.5 cm (3 in) is needed to fit over a 19 mm (¾ in) diameter rod with a 2.5 cm (1 in) frill above.

HAND-PLEATED HEADINGS

The superior results of these headings more than justify the extra time involved in making them. A professional finish is achieved in part by showing a minimum amount of stitching on the right side of the fabric.

All these headings should be stiffened. Pinch pleats are best stiffened with curtain buckram, but with most other types, strips of firm dressmaker's interfacing are quite satisfactory. Curtain buckram is available in several depths, 10 cm, 12.5 cm and 15 cm (4 in, 5 in and 6 in) and in two varieties—iron-on and standard.

Hand pinch pleat

A hand pinch pleat heading, producing sharp, crisp pleats, is far superior to a taped version. It can be pleated up to the exact length of your particular curtain fixture by adjusting the amount of fabric in each pleat and the spaces between them.

This heading is normally applied to lined curtains and is stiffened with curtain buckram.

The amount of fabric fullness required is variable and although a minimum of twice the length of the curtain fixture is satisfactory, two and a quarter to two and a half times fullness is preferable to achieve a well-balanced, attractive pleating arrangement. A minimum heading allowance of 2 cm (¾ in) plus the depth of the curtain buckram, should be added to the finished curtain length.

Several points should be borne in mind when planning your pleats:

Each curtain of a pair should have the same number of pleats.

A space of 10 cm (4 in) to 12 cm (4¾ in) between the pleats gives an attractive arrangement, but this is variable in order to arrive at the desired finished width of curtain. It is important to remember that the amount of fabric left unpleated (i.e., the total of all the spaces) must equal the length of your track (plus returns and overlap arm where applicable).

Where the curtains are to cover returns, locate one pleat at each end of the curtain fixture and leave a flat space at the outside edge of the curtain to cover the return.

When curtains are to butt together, plan to have a half space at each leading edge. When using an overlap arm, leave enough space to correspond to the size of the fitment. One complete space on each curtain is sufficient.

Finally, do not let the following calculations and precise measurements deter you. It is possible to juggle the pleating and spacing arrangements within reason, putting more or less fabric into the pleats and spaces to achieve your desired result.

To calculate the pleats-and-spacing arrangement, work on the basis of one curtain. When dealing with a pair, divide the track length in half and use this measurement when referring to track length.

Pleats As a guide start by allowing four pleats to one fabric width of 120 cm (48 in), adjusting up as necessary, particularly with wider fabric, to arrive at an attractive balance of pleats and spacing.

Subtract the track length (including return and overlap arm where applicable) from the total width of the finished flat curtain. The remainder is the amount of fabric which will be fitted into the pleats. To ascertain the amount of fabric in each pleat, divide this remaining fabric by the number of proposed pleats, using the guide above.

Spaces To establish the size of the spaces in between the pleats:

(i) *With a half space at each side of the curtain*
Divide the track length by the proposed number of pleats (fig. 3a);

or (ii) *When covering an overlap and return*
Divide the track length, excluding the amount needed to cover the overlap and return, by one less than the proposed number of pleats (fig. 3b).

For instructions on making up this heading refer to PART II Interlined Curtains.

Cartridge and goblet pleat headings
These headings need a minimum fullness of twice the track length and calculations should be treated in the same way as for pinch pleat heading, but allowing for more pleats ('tubes') of a smaller size and closer spacing. A good arrangement is to allow about 10 cm (4 in) each for a 'tube' and space in between, but vary this in order to arrive at your track length. A cartridge pleat heading is made up in the same way as pinch pleats (page 22), but the bases of the small tubes (pleats) are not pinched up but left rounded by filling with a soft stuffing such as wadding. A goblet heading (fig. 4) is made in the same way, but use a firm dressmaker's interfacing rather than curtain buckram, as the base of each tube is randomly pinched in (as opposed to pleated in) and held in position with a few hand stitches. The heading allowance is the same as for pinch pleats

Box pleat headings
This heading is quite extravagant on fabric and needs

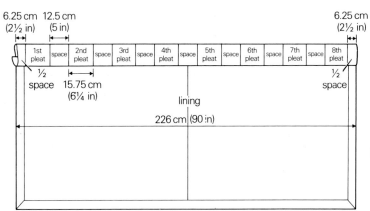

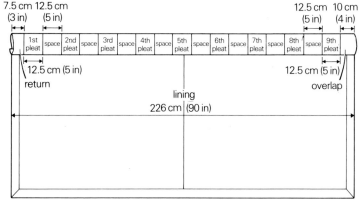

3 Pinch pleat arrangements: above *with a half space at each side to* fit a track 100 cm long without overlap; and right *using the same track length plus return of 7.5 cm and overlap of 10 cm to achieve a satisfactory balance of spacing to pleats.*

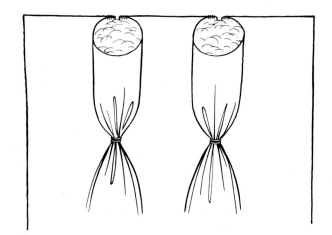

4 Goblet heading

fullness of three times the track length for true box pleats which butt up against each other. The pleats can be spaced out if preferred, needing approximately two and a half times fullness. The heading should be planned in a similar way as for pinch pleats. When planning the spacing, once again bear in mind that the total of spaces and/or the back of each pleat must equal the track length.

The size of the pleat is a matter of choice. A flattened pleat with a width of 6 cm (2⅜ in) uses 12 cm (4¾ in) of fabric plus a further 6 cm (2⅜ in) for the space behind it (fig. 5). Plan to have a flat space at either side of the curtain beyond the outer pleats for any returns.

You will need the same heading allowance as for pinch pleats if it is to be made up as a curtain heading, but for making a valance you will need only 1.5 cm (½ in) for the heading allowance.

Hand pinch pleated curtains hanging on a rod. They reflect the elegant, classic style of the room.

pinch pleat tape
curtain.

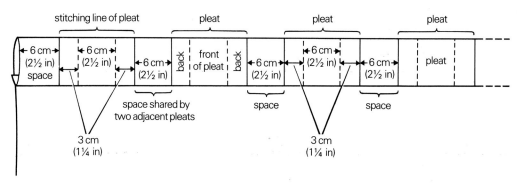

5 *Box pleat arrangement*

Scalloped headings

Scalloped headings are normally used on short café curtains and are hung below a narrow rod from rings. When the spaces between the scallops are left plain, it needs very little fabric fullness. One and a quarter fullness will enable the curtain to lie reasonably flat across the window. With pinch pleats between the scallops, a minimum of twice the pole length is necessary.

A heading allowance of 2 cm (¾ in) plus the depth of your stiffening is needed. The stiffening should be approximately 3 cm (1¼ in) deeper than one scallop.

Plain scallops Decide on the width of the scallops and the proposed width of the spaces between them. Divide the finished curtain width by the width of one scallop and space, to give the number of scallops. Add one to this figure to give the total number of spaces. bearing in mind that one extra space will be needed to balance the heading at the sides. Adjust the size of the spaces fractionally so that the total of scallops and spaces equals the width of the finished curtain.

Example Pole length 90 cm (36 in).

Using one and a quarter fullness, i.e., one width of 120 cm (48 in) wide fabric with finished curtain width of 112 cm (44 in).

Using scallop width 9 cm (3½ in) and space of 4 cm (1½ in) = 13 cm (5 in)

Divide curtain width 112 cm (44 in) by 13 (5 in)

Makes 8 scallops of 9 cm (3½ in), using 72 cm (28 in) of fabric

9 spaces of 4 cm (1½ in), using 36 cm (15½ in) of fabric

Total width—108 cm (41½ in).

Adjust by fractionally increasing size of a few spaces.

Pinch pleats between scallops This heading uses extra fullness in the spaces between the scallops. It is calculated in a similar way to ordinary pinch pleats in that the total measurement of unpleated fabric, i.e., scallops and spaces, must equal the pole length.

You will need a pleat and space at each end of the heading for balance.

Decide on the width of the scallops and allow approximately 4 cm (1½ in) per space, (which will be divided either side of each pleat when making up). Divide the pole length by the width of one scallop and space, to give the number of scallops. Add one, to give the total number of spaces.

To calculate the amount of fabric that is left for the pleats, deduct the pole length from the finished fabric width, and divide the result by the number of spaces.

Example (fig. 6) Pole length 105 cm (41½ in).

Using two and a quarter fullness, two widths of 120 cm (48 in) wide fabric will be needed, to give a finished

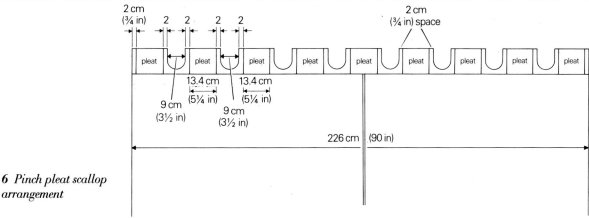

6 Pinch pleat scallop arrangement

fabric width of 226 cm (89 in).
Using scallop width of 9 cm (3½ in) and space of 4 cm (1½ in) = 13 cm (5)
Divide pole length 105 cm (41½ in) by 13 cm (5 in)
    Makes 8 scallops of 9 cm (3½ in) wide
    9 spaces of 4 cm (1½ in) wide
    Total width—108 cm (41½ in).

Fabric width 226 cm (89 in) less pole length 105 cm (41½ in) = 121 cm (47½ in) of remaining fabric to be divided between 9 spaces; this makes 13.4 cm (5¼ in) each pleat.
The total measurement of scallops and spaces is longer than the pole length, but this can be lost by increasing the size of one or two pleats.

7 MEASURING AND ESTIMATING

It is advisable to fix your track first, as it may be necessary to alter its planned position. You may decide, also, to fix a batten, in which case your track or pole will project further into the room, increasing the size of the return. Remember that unless you are fitting within a window reveal, your track should, where possible, extend beyond the sides of the window to enable the curtain to stand free of the window during daylight. The larger the curtains, the more space is required.

MEASURING
Before starting to measure, it is necessary to establish the depth of the heading, i.e., from the suspension point to the top of the curtain (fig. 7a and b). With deep-taped headings, the depth is calculated from the appropriate row of pockets to the top of the tape. With a frilled gathered heading, the depth of heading will vary according to the depth of the frill. With other hand headings, you need to decide where your curtain hooks should be positioned in order that the heading will cover the track. It may be worth making a sample heading with a little spare fabric and fitting it to the track with appropriate hooks in order to ascertain the depth needed. This point is not relevant to a pole, where the heading will hang below the suspension point (fig. 7c).

You should also decide on the length of the curtains

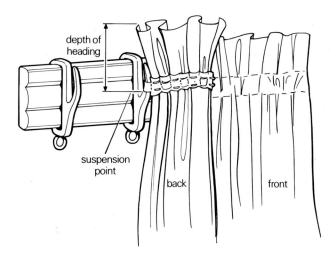

7a Depth of heading and suspension point

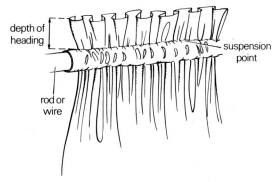

7b Channelled heading

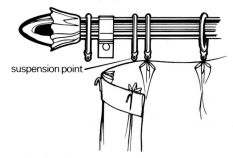

7c Heading hangs below suspension point

(fig. 8): (a) to sill, (b) just below sill, or (c) to floor. Bear in mind that in positions (a) and (c) the curtains should skirt the sill or floor to prevent undue wear and avoid soiling the hemline. Therefore, deduct a fraction from your finished length measurement unless the curtains are to act as draught excluders.

Finally, always use a metal or wooden rule for measuring as tape-measures tend to stretch and therefore are not accurate.

There are two measurements needed in order to calculate your fabric:

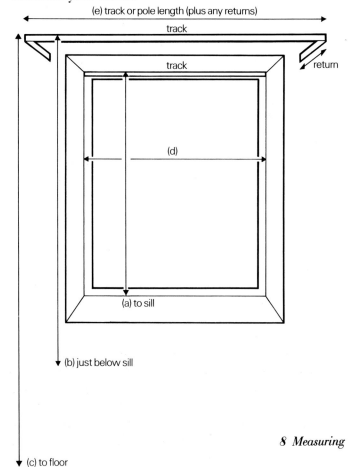

8 Measuring

Width Measure the track or pole length, excluding any finials. Add to this measurement the depth of any return(s) plus an extra 10/15 cm (4/5 in) if you have an overlap arm attached to your fitment.

Length (a) Pole—Measure from the point where your curtain will be suspended, to your chosen length.

(b) Track, rod or wire—Measure as above but *add* the depth of your chosen heading.

Measurement (a) or (b) will be your *finished length* (less an allowance for skirting the sill or floor where appropriate). Add between 20–30 cm (8–10 in) to this finished length for a double hem and a *heading allowance*. This final figure is your *cutting length*.

NB A double 7.5 cm (3 in) hem is usual. It improves the hang of curtains, and allows for shrinkage and alterations.

ESTIMATING FABRIC

In order to estimate the amount of fabric needed, you need both the measurements you have taken and a note of the width and pattern repeat of your chosen fabric.

(*1*) Multiply the total track length including return(s) and overlap by the fullness needed for your chosen heading.

(*2*) Divide this by the width of the fabric to give the number of widths of fabric required. Round off to the nearest full width, bearing in mind that although most headings are adjustable (excluding pinch and cartridge tapes), by rounding down you risk the curtains looking skimped.

(*3a*) *For plain fabrics* Multiply the number of widths by the cutting length for your total fabric requirement.

(*3b*) *For patterned fabrics* Extra fabric will be needed for matching patterns. Where there is a small pattern repeat the quickest and simplest method is to allow one full pattern repeat per width after the first width. However, when using fabric with a large pattern repeat

this can prove wasteful, so your fabric requirement should be calculated as follows:

For large pattern repeats Divide your cutting length by the size of the pattern repeat and round up to a whole number. This is the number of pattern repeats needed per drop. Multiply the number of widths by the number of pattern repeats per drop to give the total number of pattern repeats required. Multiply the total number of pattern repeats by the size of the repeat to give your total fabric requirement.

Two-part staggered patterns Calculate as above, but allow one further half pattern repeat when making a pair of curtains with more than one width in each curtain, and when complete pattern repeats are needed for each drop (fig. 9).

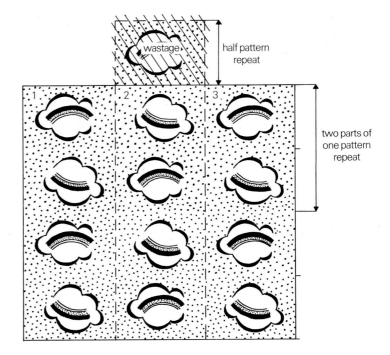

9 *Two part staggered patterns*

Any wastage from matching patterns could be used to make tie bands and cushions.

You will need the same amount of lining as outer curtain fabric, less allowance for pattern matching.

You will also need curtain heading tape or stiffening to equal the total width of your fabric. Allow a little extra for pinch pleat tape in order to balance your pleats.

When interlining curtains, you will need the same number of widths of fabric as your outer curtain, but no allowance for patterns, hems or headings is necessary.

As a guide to the number of curtain hooks you will need, allow about 4 hooks per 30 cm (12 in) on gathered headings. On pleated headings you will need one hook for every pleat and one at each side of the curtain.

Finally, you will need matching thread, plus a weight for the base of every seam and one at each corner. If you use weights in strip form you will need enough to fit the width of your hemline.

8   CUTTING OUT AND HANDLING FABRICS

Look at your fabric carefully before starting to cut out, as there are several points to observe. Give yourself plenty of room, particularly when dealing with floor-length curtains. Work on the floor if necessary.

Strictly speaking all fabrics should be cut on the straight grain. True straight grain occurs when the weft (crosswise) and warp (lengthwise) threads are at right angles to each other. This is easier to see by placing the fabric on a large rectangular table with the selvedge level with the long edge of the table. The fabric will be on grain if its width is square with the end of the table. On some fabrics it may be possible to pull a weft thread from the fabric leaving a guideline along which to cut. Problems occur on some printed fabrics when the pattern has been printed off grain. With a small print, follow the design instead of the weave so that the curtain looks right visually. A slight deviation from the grain will not affect the hang of your curtains. In bad cases, however, with large patterns, by following the pattern your curtain could be so off grain as to adversely affect its drape. On the other hand by following the grain your pattern could be on a definite slant, which would be very irritating. Unfortunately, the problem increases with multiple-width curtains. Either strike a balance between the pattern and grain or, if the problem is very bad, return the fabric before cutting.

Plain fabrics
With some plain fabrics, all drops will need to be cut in the same direction in order to match a pronounced woven design, or to ensure that fabrics with a high sheen catch the light evenly. Taffeta, pile fabrics and some dupions fall into the latter category. There are no rules as to which direction the drops should be cut. Velvets with the pile running upwards can become dust traps but some people prefer the darker, richer colour that results. With the pile running down, the colour tends to be lighter, shows fewer pressure marks, and can be brushed more easily with a downward stroke.

Patterned fabrics
It is obvious, with many patterns, in which direction the pattern should run, but others may need careful scrutiny if the top is not indicated on the selvedge of the fabric. Unbalanced stripes also have to be cut in one direction. With large patterns, aim to place the hemline at the base of a complete pattern.

Curtains with a pencil heading, caught back with tie bands, combined with a festoon blind. The combination of pole and frills creates a pretty cottagey look.

Matching patterns

With patterned fabric, the design must line up across the whole width of the curtain. To match the pattern, turn in the side of one width of fabric and line up the pattern with the width to which it will be joined. Pin, then slip-tack the two pieces together from the right side (fig. 10), making sure that the pattern does not move out of line.

Machine the seam from the wrong side over the tacking. Remove tacking and cut off the selvedge. Press seam open.

Cutting

Measure and mark off the cutting length with pins or chalk before cutting, and mark the fabric to indicate the direction of the top, where necessary. To prevent excessive fraying cut out using sharp pinking shears.

HANDLING DELICATE FABRICS

A little extra care than normal is needed when handling such fabrics as velvet, silks and fine transparent fabrics, including nets. Test a small sample of fabric for stitching, pressing and general handling prior to making up in order to obtain results free from puckering and slipping.

Velvet

Pin as little as possible as pins tend to leave marks. When pinning use needles, which are finer, and place them across the seam. Then firmly tack the seam, leaving the needles in place, to hold the layers together. The top layer of fabric tends to slip over the bottom layer while under the pressure foot, so carefully machine the seam over the needles and tacking, following the direction of the nap (i.e., the direction in which the pile is lying).

Velvet drapes beautifully, so it is acceptable to use a single mitred hem, which will lie flatter, particularly as it cannot be pressed. In this instance, you must finish off the raw edge of the hem either by overcasting or, for a

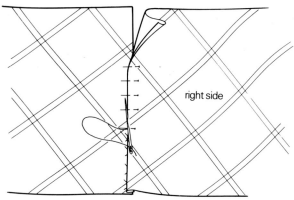

10 *Sliptacking*

really professional finish, by binding it with a fine bias binding.

Pressing is difficult with pile fabrics. It is advisable not to press the seams at all unless you have a needle board (a length of canvas covered with fine, shallow wires into which the pile side of the fabric is pressed). It is possible to use a spare piece of velvet as a substitute so that the pile of the fabric you are working on sinks into the pile of the spare piece underneath. The point of the iron should then be applied very gently to the seam only. I cannot emphasize enough the amount of care needed in this process, so if you are in any doubt about the outcome, do not attempt it. Newly hung velvet may show creases and pressure marks but as the pile and lustre returns these will drop out.

Fine fabrics

These include silks, transparent fabrics and nets. Use very sharp, fine pins (or needles), and very sharp scissors when handling these lightweight materials to prevent snagging the fine threads and puckering the fabric. Try to keep the fabric absolutely flat when cutting out. Use a padded weight to anchor the fabric to the table to prevent it slipping. Place the pins across seams. Fine fabrics are more easily stitched when tacked to tissue paper, which can be torn away afterwards. Use fine thread; silk thread with silk fabrics, and synthetic thread with synthetic fabrics. Transparent fabrics require neat seams as they can be seen from the right side. Narrow french, or mock french, seams should be used, or a narrow plain seam with the seam allowances finished off together with a zig-zag stitch. Make double hems where extra weight is needed and provided it looks right visually. Alternatively, make a narrow double-stitched hem (page 38).

9 BASIC SEWING TECHNIQUES

Whatever you plan to make, the contents of this chapter will be useful. It is worth remembering that 'practice makes perfect'. Once you have made yourself familiar with the basic sewing processes, you will then be able to cope with any of the projects in this book.

STITCHES

Basting (tacking) is a temporary stitch used to hold layers of fabric together (fig. 11).

Drawstitch is used to join two folded edges together (fig 12).

Hemming is used to hold a folded edge against another layer of fabric (fig. 13).

Herringbone stitch is generally used to hold a single turned edge securely in position against a single layer of fabric (fig. 14).

Lockstitch is used to loosely hold linings to curtains and is like a long loose blanket stitch. It is worked from between the curtain and the lining (fig. 15).

Overcast (oversewing) is used to neaten raw edges to prevent them from fraying (fig. 16).

Serging is used to hold a single turning in place on the sides of the curtains. It is like a large hemming stitch and must not show on the right side (fig. 17).

Slipstitch should be invisible from both sides and is used to hold a folded edge in place (fig. 18).

Stabstitch is a tiny, almost invisible stitch, and is used to attach trimming to materials (fig. 19).

Seams

For the inexperienced, it is advisable to pin and tack before permanently hand or machine stitching seams.

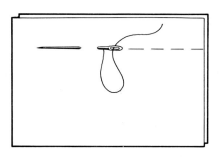

11 Tacking

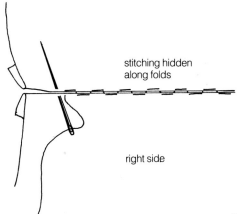

stitching hidden
along folds

right side

12 Drawstitch

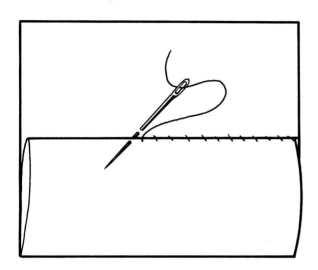

13 Hemming

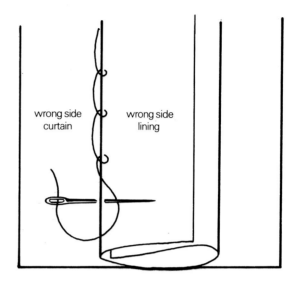

wrong side curtain

wrong side lining

15 Lockstitch

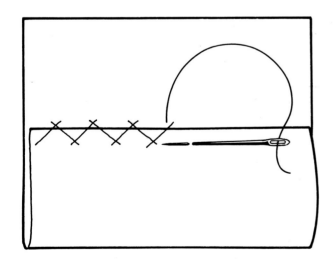

14 Herringbone

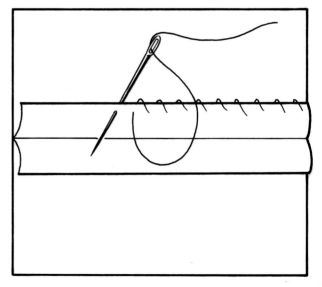

16 Overcast

Roller blinds are well suited to a modern room.

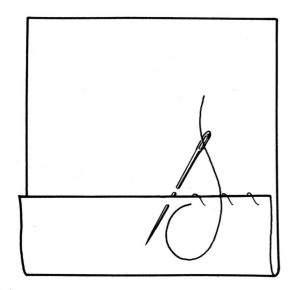

17 Serge

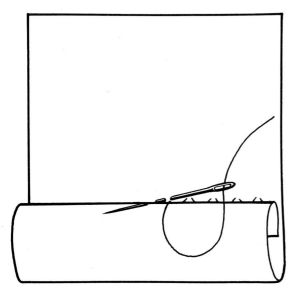

18 Slipstitch

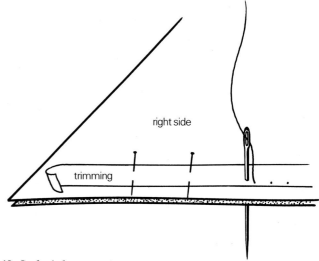

19 Stabstitch

Plain open seam is inconspicuous from the right side and is the most widely used, with an average-sized seam allowance of 1.5 cm (⅝ in). To make a plain seam, place two pieces of fabric together with right sides facing and with raw edges level. Pin on the seamline, 1.5 cm (⅝ in) in from the raw edges, with pins placed at right angles to the seam. Less fabric is taken up when they are placed at this angle, preventing the seamline from reducing and puckering. Tack the seamline and remove pins (fig. 20), then machine. To press the seam, first press the seam allowances together on the wrong side to embed the stitches in the fabric, then press the seam open. The seam allowances should be neatened, when not covered by a lining, with a machine zig-zag over the raw edges, or by overcasting.

The seam allowances of the following seams are self-neatened by enclosing them in the seam itself, and are therefore useful when making unlined curtains.

Flat fell seam is a neat, strong seam. Stitch a plain

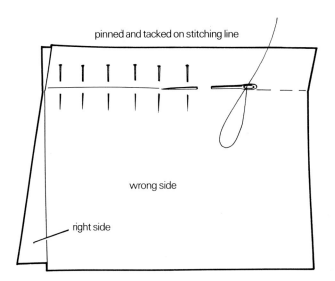

20 Plain open seam

seam on the wrong side of the fabric. Press the seam allowance to one side. Trim the under seam allowance to 3 mm (⅛ in). Turn under the raw edge of the top seam allowance and tack in place over the trimmed edge. Topstitch close to fold. Alternatively, to prevent any stitching being seen from the right side, slipstitch the top edge in place (fig. 21).

French seam is used on lightweight, sheer fabrics where a strong, narrow seam is required. No stitching is visible from the right side. With wrong sides facing, stitch 6 mm (¼ in) from the seamline within the seam allowance. Press seam allowances together. Trim seam to 3 mm (⅛ in). Turn right sides together; fold and press on the stitching line. Stitch another row of stitches on the seamline to enclose the raw edges (fig. 22).

It is not possible to match a large defined pattern in the normal way (page 32) with this seam as the first row of stitching is carried out with wrong sides facing. It would therefore be easier to restrict this seam to plain fabrics or those with a small overall design.

Mock French seam is a type of french seam which is quicker to achieve. Stitch a plain seam with right sides together. Turn in the raw edges of both seam allowances towards each other and match the folded edges. Stitch the turned edges close to the fold (fig. 23).

HEMS

As mentioned earlier, curtains should have good-sized hems. Mitres are folded at the corners of hems to distribute the bulk of fabric evenly and neatly. Never cut off the excess fabric across the corner or you will not be able to let the curtain down.

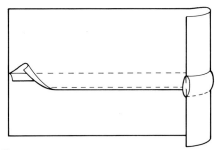

21 Flat fell seam

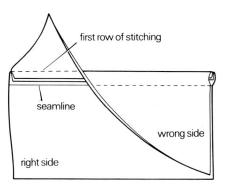

22 French seam

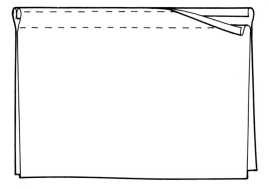

23 Mock French seam

and hem or slipstitch the remainder of the hem.

Narrow double-stitched hem is suitable for fine light-weight fabrics to finish off single-sided frills. Machine 5 mm (¼ in) away from the raw edge with small stitches. Turn under 5 mm (¼ in) to the wrong side on machined line. Then turn 5 mm (¼ in) again. Machine in position.

Double plain hem with mitred corner is used with all lined curtains (fig. 24). A finished hem of 7.5 cm (3 in) is generally sufficient. To make this hem, turn and press approximately 4 cm (1½ in) to the wrong side along each side of the curtain and press; then open out. Turn up 15 cm (6 in) hem allowance and press to mark the hemline. Turn it back down again to reveal the corner between the creased hemline and sides. Fold the fabric diagonally through the corner of the hemline and sides of curtain. Turn in the sides again and make the first 7.5 cm (3 in) fold in the hem. Then make a second 7.5 cm (3 in) turning so that the diagonal folds meet. Pin in place and stitch the folds of the mitre with a drawstitch

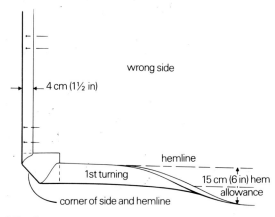

24b Mitred corner

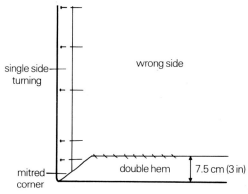

24a Double hem with mitred corners

24c Complete mitred corner

PART II

10 UNLINED CURTAINS
With gathered taped heading and a detachable lining.

Unlined curtains are ideal when made up in easy-care fabrics which can be laundered frequently, making them perfect for kitchens or bathrooms. Reversible fabrics are good where no lining is used at all, making the curtains as attractive from the outside as inside. A detachable lining which can be removed and washed separately need not use the same fullness as the outer curtain; one and a half times the track length can be sufficient. A special lining tape is available which has two flaps of tape running along one edge, between which the top of the lining is sandwiched.

MAKING UP
(Refer to Chapter 6, 7 and 8.)
Cut out the required number of drops, matching the pattern where appropriate. Cut off the selvedges completely to remove the tension along these tight edges. This will prevent the seam from tightening up with the result that it could be shorter than the surrounding fabric. Join the widths together, matching any pattern, with a mock French or flat fell seam (page 37). Press seam. Place any half or part widths to the outer edges of the curtain, when making a pair, so that you have a left and a right hand curtain.

Sides Make a double 2 cm (¾ in) turning to the wrong side along each side of the curtains. Pin and tack to hold in position. The width of the side hems can be varied to suit the thickness of fabric. Either machine these side hems, or slipstitch by hand.

Hems Turn up, then pin a double 7.5 cm (3 in) hem (a double 5 cm (2 in) hem is sufficient for short length curtains). Stitch a weight inside the hem at each corner and at the base of each seam. Tack hem, then slipstitch. Drawstitch the sides of the hem together.

Heading
Lay the curtains out flat. Measure up from the hemline and mark the finished length of the curtains, either by tacking across the width of the fabric, or with a row of pins on the right side. Turn the 4 cm (1½ in) heading allowance to the wrong side along the tacked line indicating the top edge of the curtains. Pin and tack to hold. Cut a length of standard gathering tape approximately 8 cm (3 in) longer than the width of the finished curtain. Pull out 4 cm (1½ in) of cord from one end and knot. Trim the tape to within 1 cm (⅜ in) of knot, then turn it under. Position this end at the leading edge, pinning the tape over the raw edge of the turned down heading allowance, and leaving 2.5 cm (1 in) above it (fig. 25). At the other end of the tape pull out 4 cm (1½ in) of cords and leave free for gathering up later. Trim the tape to 1 cm (⅜ in), turn under then pin and tack it to the outside edge of the curtain. Machine the tape close to its edge, avoiding the cords, stitching along

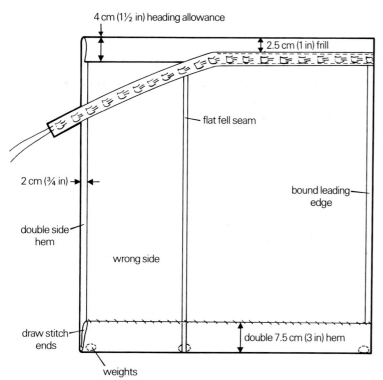

4 cm (1½ in) heading allowance

2.5 cm (1 in) frill

flat fell seam

2 cm (¾ in)

bound leading edge

double side hem

wrong side

draw stitch ends

double 7.5 cm (3 in) hem

weights

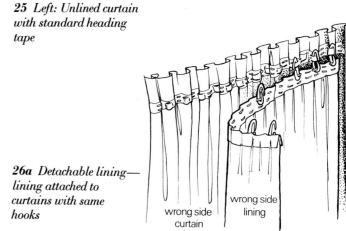

25 *Left: Unlined curtain with standard heading tape*

26a *Detachable lining— lining attached to curtains with same hooks*

wrong side curtain

wrong side lining

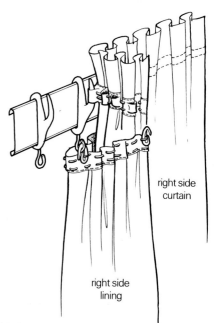

right side curtain

right side lining

26b *Lining attached to base of hook/glider*

the top and bottom in the same direction. Pull up the tape, tying the cords neatly, and spread the gathers evenly.

DETACHABLE LINING

This lining can be fitted to the outer curtain by hanging it from the same curtain hooks (fig. 26a), or from the base of the glider on a track with combined hook/gliders (fig. 26b). When fitting as in fig. 26a, cut the lining to the finished length of the curtain, less 2.5 cm (1 in) to clear the hemline, less a further 4 cm (1½ in) for the depth of the heading, but include a double hem allowance. When fitting as in fig. 26b deduct a further 2.5 cm (1 in) to allow for the distance between the hook of the glider and the top of the lining.

Make up the lining in the same way as the curtains, but machine all hems. Cut a length of lining tape approximately 8 cm (3 in) longer than the finished width of the lining. Pull out 4 cm (1½ in) of cords from one end and knot them together. Trim 2 cm (¾ in) from the tape. Position this end to the leading edges of the lining. Repeat at the other end but leave the cords free. Sandwich the top of the lining between the two layers of the tape, turning the ends over twice to bring them level with the sides of the lining (fig. 27). Pin and tack the tape in position. Machine along the bottom edge of the tape, trapping the lining, and across the ends to neaten them off.

Pull up the lining to fit the size of the outer curtain and insert the curtain hooks, first into the lining tape then into the standard tape on the curtains to hang them on a conventional track. In the case of fig. 26b, slot the curtain hook on the lining into the hole at the base of the hook/glider.

The sides of the lining can be temporarily hand stitched to the sides of the curtain, if desired.

27 Lining sandwiched between two flaps of lining tape

11   LINED CURTAINS
With deep taped heading.

A lining not only protects the curtain fabric from sunlight but when sewn in as opposed to being detachable, it also improves the hang of the curtains. Coloured lining looks attractive from the outside and can also be displayed in the room during daytime as a contrast to the curtains by draping the curtains back in tie bands and turning the leading edges into the room.

MAKING UP
(Refer to Chapter 6, 7 and 8.)
Cut out the required number of drops of curtain fabric, matching the pattern where appropriate. Join the widths with a plain seam, placing any part widths to the outer edges of the curtains. It is acceptable to snip the selvedges approximately every 10 cm (4 in) to release the tension on a plain seam. Press the seams open.

Mark the hemline on the curtain fabric by turning up the 15 cm (6 in) hem allowance to the wrong side, and press. Lay the curtains out flat and measure up from the creased hemline to mark the finished length of the curtains (top edge) with a row of tacking stitches across the width of the curtain.

Sides
Make a single 4 cm (1½ in) turning to the wrong sides on each side of the curtains. Pin turning, then hold it in

place with a large herringbone stitch or serging, (page 33) stopping approximately 25 cm (10 in) from the bottom edge in order to complete mitred corners.

Hem

Turn up and pin a double 7.5 cm (3 in) hem on creased hemline, folding mitres at each corner (page 38). Stitch weights in the hem at the base of each seam and at each corner. Complete the hem by slipstitching.

Complete herringbone stitching at the lower part of side seams, above the mitres.

Lining

Cut the lining as for the outer fabric and join the widths together in the same way. Turn up and pin a double 7.5 cm (3 in) hem, then machine it in place.

Lay the curtain out flat with wrong side uppermost. Lay the lining on top with wrong sides facing and with its hemline 2.5 cm (1 in) above the curtain hemline.

Turn the sides of the lining back and lockstitch (page 33) lining to the wrong side of the curtain from top to bottom on all seams, and along the middle of each width (fig. 28). Smooth the lining out flat again, then turn in the sides of the lining and pin it to the curtains, leaving a 2.5 cm (1 in) margin of curtain fabric showing at each side. While the curtain is laid out flat, pin and tack the lining to the curtain along the marked top edge of the curtain. Slipstitch the lining in place along the sides and continue round the hemline for approximately 2.5 cm (1 in).

Attaching a deep heading tape

Lay the curtains out flat with lining sides uppermost. Trim the lining to the same level as the curtain at the top. Turn the 1.5 cm (½ in) heading allowance to the wrong side on marked top edge of curtain. Pin and tack in place.

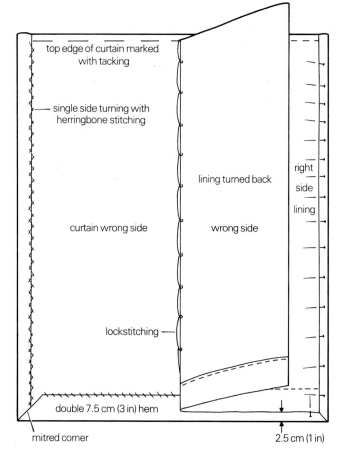

top edge of curtain marked with tacking

single side turning with herringbone stitching

lining turned back

right side lining

curtain wrong side

wrong side

lockstitching

double 7.5 cm (3 in) hem

mitred corner

2.5 cm (1 in)

28 Locking lining to curtains

Cut a length of tape approximately 8 cm (3 in) longer than the finished width of the curtain. Pull out approximately 4 cm (1½ in) of cord from each end. (It may be necessary to pick these out with a pin on pinch pleat and cartridge tapes if you are not cutting between the pleats.) Tie knots in the cords at one end, and if using pencil pleat tape trim the tape only to within 1.5 cm (½ in) of knot. Place this end to the leading edges of the curtains, turning in the ends of the tape. With pinch and cartridge pleat tape you will need to balance your end spaces to make your pleating symmetrical on both curtains. You will, therefore, have to vary the amount of tape turned under. Pin the tape to the curtain over the heading allowance, fractionally down from the top of the curtain (fig. 29). Turn in the other end of the tape, leaving the cords free for pulling up. Pin, then machine the tape in place, making sure you stitch the top and bottom row in the same direction.

Pull up the tape to fit the track; tie the cords neatly and insert curtain hooks.

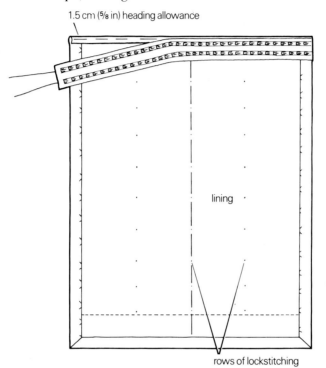

1.5 cm (⅝ in) heading allowance

lining

rows of lockstitching

29 *Attaching deep heading tape*

12   INTERLINED CURTAINS
With hand pinch pleat heading.

These curtains make excellent draught excluders and give extra insulation. Interlining will add years to the life of your curtains and you are likely to tire of them well before they wear out. The stiffness of a hand pleated heading will help to keep the heading crisp and firm, giving a truly professional finish. Curtains are normally interlined with bump, but other soft fabrics can be used.

MAKING UP
(Refer to Chapter 6, 7 and 8.)
This method gives a less bulky finish to the hem. If a thick, weighty hem is preferred, however, interlining can

be cut to the exact size of the outer curtain, excluding the heading allowance, but you will need slightly more fabric to allow for a hem allowance. Once the interlining has been locked in, the two layers of fabric can be treated as one and made up in the same way.

Cut out the required number of drops of curtain fabric and lining to your cutting length as calculated, and join matching the pattern where appropriate, as with lined curtains. Turn up and pin a double 7.5 cm (3 in) hem on the lining and machine it in place.

Cut out the same number of widths of interlining to the finished curtain length. To keep the seams as flat as possible, join the widths by overlapping the selvedges by approximately 1.5 cm (½ in) then zig-zag two rows of stitching, each row catching a raw edge (fig. 30).

Mark the hemline and finished top edge of the curtains as with lined curtains. Also mark the finished side edges by turning in 6 cm (2½ in) to the wrong side and press. Open out all turnings after pressing.

Attaching interlining

Lay curtain fabric out flat with wrong side uppermost. Lay the interlining on top with the raw edges of interlining level with the marked hemline and top edge of the curtains (fig. 31). Fold the interlining back and lockstitch it to the wrong side of the curtains in the same way as for the lining in Lined Curtains, but stitch two vertical rows for each width of fabric at equal distances apart and along all seams. Smooth the interlining back and tack the outer edges of bump to the sides of the curtain all around.

Sides and hem

Finish off the sides by turning them in to the wrong side on the creaselines, with the interlining. Take the curtain hem allowance over the cut edge of interlining, and complete the sides and hem with mitred corners (page 38).

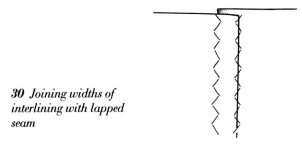

30 Joining widths of interlining with lapped seam

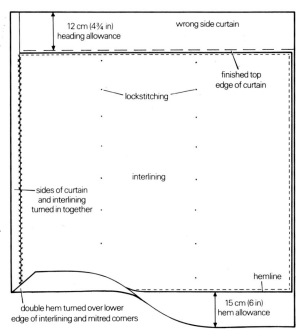

12 cm (4¾ in) heading allowance

wrong side curtain

finished top edge of curtain

lockstitching

interlining

sides of curtain and interlining turned in together

hemline

double hem turned over lower edge of interlining and mitred corners

15 cm (6 in) hem allowance

31 Attaching interlining

Lining

Lay the curtain out flat with the interlining uppermost and apply the hemmed lining to it in the same way as for Lined Curtains, but lockstitching along the same lines as the interlining and along all seams.

Hand pinch pleat heading

Cut a length of 10 cm (4 in) deep curtain buckram to the finished width of the curtain. Lay the curtain out flat with the lining uppermost. Place the buckram over the heading allowance with its lower edge level with the marked top edge of the curtain. Turn the top 2 cm (¾ in) of curtain and lining over the top edge of the buckram, then tack and machine it in place close to the folded edge (fig. 32). Turn the buckram down to the wrong side on the marked top edge of the curtain and tack it in place.

Plan your pleating arrangement as on page 22–3. On the wrong side of the heading, mark your calculated pleats and spaces with tailor's chalk, or with rows of pins on the right side (fig. 33). Fold each pleat by bringing the marked sides of each pleat together on the wrong side. Tack each pleat in place on the right side, from top to bottom of buckram. When all the pleats have been tacked, check the finished curtain width and adjust as necessary, bearing in mind that the total finished width of both curtains must equal the track length. Machine the pleats over the tacking, using a reverse machine stitch to start and finish the stitching, for security. Remove the tacking. At the sides of the curtain, machine a double row of stitching, 5 mm (¼ in) apart, along the depth of the heading.

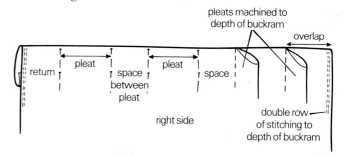

33 *Making pleats*

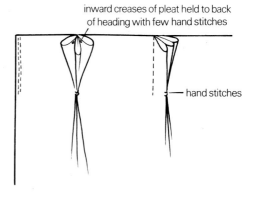

32 *Attaching curtain buckram to heading allowance*

34 *Pleat pinched into three sections*

Forming the pinch pleats Hold the centre of the single pleat and press it towards the stitching line behind, to form three separate pleats of equal size. Hold the pleats in place by oversewing a few hand stitches at the base of each pleat (fig. 34). Also hold the inward creases of the pleat to the back of the heading with a few hand stitches at the top of the pleat. Insert pin hooks at the appropriate depth into the back of each pleat, taking care not to break the thread, and at each side of the curtain.

Hanging
Hang the curtains by inserting one curtain hook into each glider on track or pole and draw the curtains back into an open position. If fitting to a track pull the spaces between the pleats forward, but if fitting to a pole, gently push the spaces back. Position the folds in the fabric which form below each pleat by running your fingers down the length of the curtain. The drape of the fabric will improve if the curtain is left like this for a while.

13   CAFÉ CURTAINS

A café curtain is an ideal way of giving privacy if you are overlooked, or for blocking out an unwanted view, as this type of curtain covers the lower half of the window permanently, leaving the top half uncovered.

It is normally unlined and made as one short curtain rather than as a pair. It can have one of several headings; a frilled channelled heading can be fitted onto a narrow rod or it can hang below a rod from rings with a plain or pinch pleated scalloped heading. It could be teamed with an additional short pair of curtains hung from the top of the window to create a tiered effect. These could be drawn to give further privacy at night.

TO MAKE A CAFÉ CURTAIN WITH PLAIN SCALLOPED HEADING
(Refer to Chapters 6, 7 and 8.)
Allow for a double 5 cm (2 in) hem. You will also need strips of iron-on dressmaker's interfacing to stiffen the heading to equal the finished width of your curtain fabric by the depth of the scallop plus 3 cm (1¼ in).

Firstly, you will need to make a card template for your scallops in order to mark them off accurately. Draw a circle with a diameter equal to the width of your scallop,

then draw a horizontal line across the diameter. At each end of the line draw a vertical line upwards to equal the radius of the circle. Then join the top of these two vertical lines with another horizontal line (fig. 35). If you would like deeper scallops, extend the length of the two vertical lines to suit. Cut round the outline.

Cut the required number of widths of fabric and join them as for unlined curtains (page 39). Cut strips of interfacing to equal the width of the curtain fabric less the

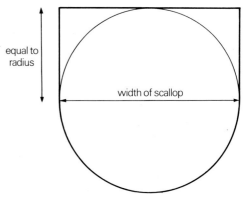

35 Template for scallop

side hems, by the depth of the scallop plus 3 cm (1¼ in). Turn in the 4 cm (1½ in) side hem allowance and press it to mark. Open out. Mark the finished top edge of the curtain by measuring down the depth of the heading allowance (interfacing plus 2 cm (¾ in)) and tack a line across the curtain at this depth. Iron the interfacing to the wrong side of the heading allowance, with its lower edge level with the marked top of the curtain and its ends touching the creaseline of the sides. Turn the top 2 cm (¾ in) down over the interfacing, then pin and machine it in place (fig. 36). Fold the sides, hem in place and treat as for Unlined Curtains, but making a double 5 cm (2 in) hem.

Turn the heading allowance to the right side on marked top edge of curtain and pin in position temporarily. This heading allowance also acts as a facing. Mark the position of the scallops with chalk on the interfacing, using the template. Tack round the marked scallops, through the facing and curtain, then machine. Trim the fabric away inside the scallops, cutting close to the stitching line and notching out the seam allowance round the curves (fig. 37). Turn the facing to the wrong side and press. Drawstitch the ends of the facing and curtain together along the sides.

TO MAKE A SCALLOPED PINCH-PLEATED HEADING
(Refer to Chapter 6, 7 and 8)
Complete the curtains in the same way as above, having left larger spaces between the scallops for pleating, as calculated. On the wrong side of the heading (facing), mark the position of the pleats as planned, remembering that the total measurement of all the scallops plus the spaces either side of each pleat must equal the length of the pole (fig. 6, page 27). Make up the pinch pleats as Interlined Curtains, leaving a tiny space on either side of the pleats (fig. 38).

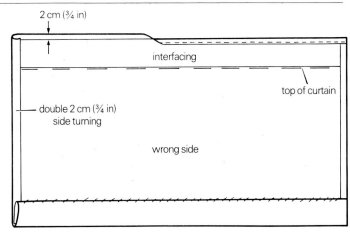

36 Interfacing on wrong side of heading allowance

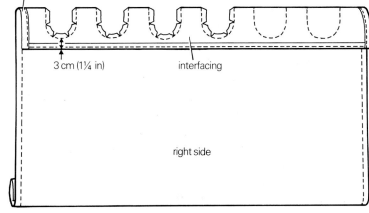

37 Facing (heading allowance) turned to right side: scallops marked, stitched and cut out

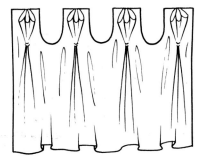

38 Finished pinch pleat scallop

14 PELMETS

A fabric-covered pelmet can give a neat finish to the top of curtains, and at the same time conceal any unattractive tracks. A shaped edge will soften its general appearance and, trimmed with braid or fringing, it will suit a traditional, formal setting. Its success depends largely on its proportions to the accompanying curtains and surroundings. A deep pelmet in a room with a low ceiling can have a heavy effect, increasing the problem. A depth of between one-sixth and one-eighth of the overall curtain length will give a good proportion, but this will depend upon individual shapes of windows and should vary accordingly.

Pelmet buckram, available in 90 cm (36 in) and 45 cm (18 in) widths, is used to stiffen the fabric cover. It is impregnated with glue, and fabric can be ironed on when dampened. The stiffened cover is fitted to a pelmet board—like a three-sided shelf—to give it support. The board can be made up in 25 mm (1 in) thick softwood to a length fractionally longer than the curtain track, to allow access to fix the track and hang the curtains (fig. 39). The depth of the shelf from the wall should be a minimum of 10 cm (4 in) to allow room for the track and bulk of fabric when the curtains are drawn back. The frame can be fitted to the wall outside the window reveal with a number of angle brackets spaced evenly along its length. The curtain track is fitted either to the underside of the board towards the back, or to the wall. The stiffened cover can be fitted to the board either with touch-and-close fastener; or with drawing pins inserted through pockets on webbing tape, stitched to the back; or tacked directly onto the board with steel tacks, provided the tacks are covered with braid.

A selection of designs is shown in fig. 40. When choosing a shape, consider any pattern on your fabric and select a shape to blend with the design. Try to avoid

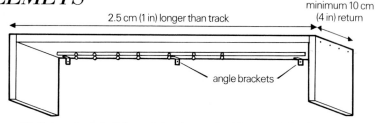

39 Pelmet board with track fitted to underside towards back

angular prints on a pelmet with a highly curved edge, as the designs could conflict. Any pattern on the accompanying curtains should unite with that on the pelmet.

It is advisable to make a paper pattern for all shaped pelmets. Measure the front edge of the pelmet board plus the two returns. You will need a strip of paper to equal this length by at least the desired depth of your pelmet. Fold the paper in half, and taking the fold as the centre of the pelmet, mark the position of the return on the opposite end. Draw half the pattern between the fold of paper and the beginning of the return, leaving the latter plain. Cut round the design through the double thickness of paper. Open out the pattern and place it in position at the window to check its proportions.

For a scalloped design, after deciding upon the number of scallops needed, divide the paper into the same number of equal sections, excluding the returns. Make a template of the scallop (see Café Curtains, page 46) or use an appropriately sized plate, to mark them off accurately.

To calculate your fabric requirements, you will need a strip(s) of outer fabric and lining to equal the length and depth of your pattern, plus a 2.5 cm (1 in) turning allowance all round, plus extra for matching a pattern. You will need pelmet buckram and bump to equal the exact size of your pattern. For fixing your pelmet, allow

The pattern of the fabric has been used to create an unusual pelmet design.

either enough touch-and-close fastener, or 4 cm (1½ in) deep webbing tape to fit the length of the board plus two returns. For trimming, allow enough braid to go round the pelmet outline, or fringing for the bottom line of pelmet only.

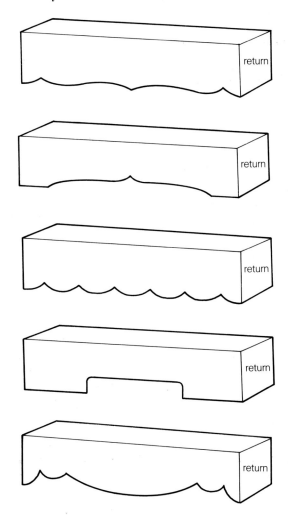

40 *Selection of pelmet shapes*

MAKING UP

Cut out the buckram and bump to the exact pattern size. Iron pattern to the buckram for ease, and cut with sharp scissors. Cut out the pelmet fabric and lining to the pattern shape with a 2.5 cm (1 in) allowance all round. If your pelmet is wider than one width of fabric, and to avoid an obvious central seam, you should make joins on the pelmet fabric and lining either side of a central panel, with a plain seam pressed open, and match any pattern. Join widths of bump, if necessary, with an overlapped seam (see page 44).

Dampen the edges on one side of the buckram, lay the bump on top, and press (not iron) with a damp cloth and warm iron to adhere.

Reinforce the turning line of the pelmet fabric and lining, 2.5 cm (1 in) in from raw edge, on inward corners, such as between scallops, with a row of small machine stitches.

Lay the pelmet fabric out flat with wrong sides uppermost. Then lay buckram on top, with bump sandwiched in between and with a 2.5 cm (1 in) border of fabric showing all round. Dampen the edge of the buckram and bring the turning allowance of pelmet fabric over, and press with an iron to bond together, snipping the allowance to the reinforcement stitching on inward corners, and around all other curves to allow the fabric to spread. Notch out fabric on inner curves to reduce bulk and enable the fabric to lie flat. Remove tacking.

Stabstitch braid to the outline of the pelmet on right side at this stage, but stitch fringing to the lower edge of the pelmet when the pelmet has been completed, or fix with fabric adhesive.

Depending on your method of fixing, *either:* pin and machine the soft side of touch-and-close fastener to the right side of the lining along the top, 2.5 cm (1 in) in from the cut edge; *or* pin a length of webbing tape in the same position turning in the ends of the tape. Machine down the ends and along the lower edge; then stitch vertically every 8 cm (3 in) to form pockets in the tape (fig. 41).

Pin the lining to the pelmet with wrong sides facing, turning in the allowance after snipping and notching out as on the pelmet fabric (fig. 41). Slipstitch in position. In order that the method of fixing is secured to the pelmet buckram and not only to the lining, hand stitch, with a strong needle and thread, along the previous machine stitching on the tape, catching the buckram but not allowing the stitches to show on the right side.

Finally, to attach the pelmet to the board, either attach the firm side of the touch-and-close fastener to the top edge of the board with steel tacks, if using the first method above, or place a strong drawing pin through each pocket on the tape and into the top edge of the board, bending the returns round the ends of the board.

NB When using pile fabrics which cannot be ironed in the same way, cut the bump 2.5 cm (1 in) larger than the buckram all round. Then apply the interlining to the

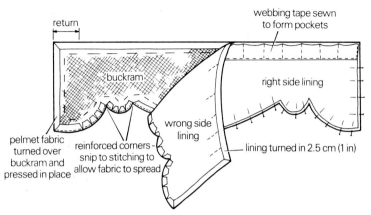

41 *Buckram covered with face fabric and lining*

buckram by pressing the bump turning allowance to the back, as with the pelmet fabric described above. Then serge (page 34) the turning allowance of the outer fabric to the turning of the interlining on the back of the pelmet and through the buckram, making sure no stitches show on the right side.

15 VALANCES

A soft, pretty valance will give a feminine, romantic finish to the top of curtains, and at the same time hide those unattractive fixtures and fittings. They can be gathered or pleated with most headings, provided the depth of the heading is in proportion to the depth of the valance. Individual touches can be added by shaping the hemline, or by binding the top and bottom edges with fabric in a contrasting or toning colour. They should be lined and/or interlined to match accompanying curtains.

The depth of the valance should be in proportion to the accompanying curtains, as with a pelmet. Here again, allow one-sixth to one-eighth of the overall curtain length, but bear in mind individual window shapes.

Valances can be fitted in one of several ways. There are a few tracks available which combine with a valance rail (page 16). Valance or curtain hooks, inserted into the heading, are then simply hooked over the rail. Alternatively, a 25 mm (1 in) thick wooden shelf can be fitted inside or outside a window reveal with angle brackets, into which staples or screw-eyes can be fixed along the front edge and returns. These metal loops should be spaced to correspond with the curtain hooks on the heading (fig. 42).

To estimate your fabric and lining requirements, you will need to measure the length of the valance rail, or shelf, plus returns. Decide upon the depth of the valance and calculate as for curtains (page 29), but add only 4 cm (1½ in) for a single hem plus 1.5 cm (⅝ in) heading allowance.

You will also need curtain heading tape or stiffening of your choice (Chapter 6) to the length of your valance strip, plus enough valance or curtain hooks to space approximately every 7.5 cm (3 in) along a gathered heading, or one for each pleat on a pleated heading, and one for each end.

TO MAKE A LINED BOX-PLEATED VALANCE

Cut the required number of widths of fabric and join them to make one long strip with a plain open seam and matching any pattern. Press seam open. Repeat for the lining, but cut each width 2.5 cm (1 in) shorter. After joining the lining widths, trim the sides so that the total width is 10 cm (4 in) less than the total width of valance.

Turn a single 4 cm (1½ in) turning to the wrong side on the valance sides and hem, mitring the corners (page 38). Press, then open out. Pin a length of curtain buckram or strips of softer stiffening to the wrong side across the whole width of the valance between the creasemark of the sides, and positioned 1.5 cm (½ in)

down from the cut top edge. Tack in place all round, or iron on, according to the type of stiffening used. Turn the top 1.5 cm (½ in) heading allowance down over the stiffening and tack in place. Turn in the sides on the creaselines, over the ends of the stiffening. Serge (page 33), or herringbone, the sides in place, above the mitred corner (fig. 43).

Turn 1.5 cm (½ in) to the wrong side along the sides and top edge of the lining and press. With right sides facing, pin the hem of the valance to the bottom of the lining, taking a 1.5 cm (½ in) seam between the diagonal lines of the mitre (fig. 24). Turn lining to the wrong side by folding the valance up on the creased hemline, re-folding the mitres so that 2.5 cm (1 in) of valance fabric shows below the lining, and the top edges are level. Pin sides of lining to sides of valance, leaving a 2.5 cm (1 in) margin of valance fabric showing. Slip-stitch lining and mitres in place. Pin top edges of valance and lining together and drawstitch the folded edges together.

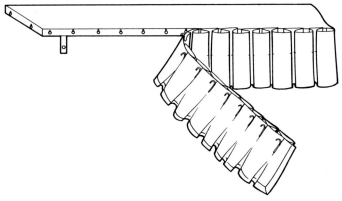

42 One method of fixing a valance

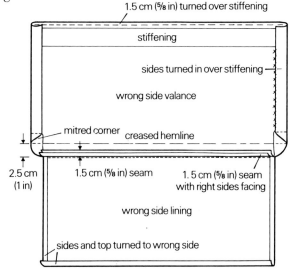

43 Attaching lining to hem of valance

An original style of valance, fitted to a pelmet board. The sides have been pleated up and the fabric caught up in the centre to form two swags.

Box pleats

On the wrong side, mark off your pleats and spaces with tailors chalk, as calculated on pages 23–26, and 45, fig. 33, to the depth of stiffening, leaving a space between the pleats if preferred. Draw solid lines on either side of each pleat, indicating those that will be stitched together, and tack through the heading to indicate the fold lines of each pleat. Pin and tack the pleats on the right side from top of valance to bottom of stiffening, by bringing the solid lines together on the wrong side as with pinch pleats (fig. 33). When all the pleats have been tacked in place, check that the finished width equals the length of the valance rail. Machine over tacking, then remove tacking. Press each pleat flat on the tacked fold lines. Catch both top corners of each pleat to the heading behind with a few hand stitches and also at the base of the stiffening, to hold in position (fig. 44). Insert a curtain pin hook into the back of each pleat and at sides.

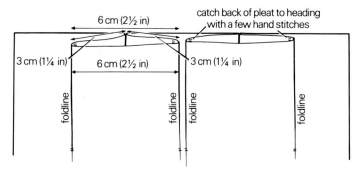

44 Box pleats

16   SWAGS AND TAILS

Swags and tails are an elegant form of heading which suit a large room with a classical, formal décor. They will add a sumptuous air to your curtains, particularly when made up in soft, supple fabrics which drape beautifully. Lining the tails with fabric of a contrasting colour will show on the graduated ends, and edging the whole creation with a braid or fringe trimming will add a splendid finish.

They are normally made by professionals in a workroom, and depend on a skill in handling and arranging fabric to achieve the best possible folds and drape in the fabric. There is no reason why these should not be made in the home provided the design is kept to a simple one for a first attempt.

Many of these headings are cut on the bias to improve the drape of the fabric, but this requires more skill to achieve and is also more extravagant on fabric. Several swags can be positioned across a large window, but do not attempt this until you are more experienced.

It is well worth experimenting with a cheap soft fabric, such as mull. You can then use the result as your cutting pattern and to estimate your fabric and lining requirements.

Avoid velvet, as it is difficult to handle. Large-patterned fabrics will loose their appeal when combined in a complex swag, and should certainly be avoided for bias-cut swags. The latter should be made up in plain fabrics or those with a small overall design.

The restrained style of this swag and tails is in keeping with the simple décor of the bedroom.

Swags and tails are an elaborate form of valance and as such should be in proportion to their accompanying curtains. As a guide, the depth of the swag and inner edges of the tails should be approximately one sixth the overall curtain length, but the outer edge of the tails should be at least twice this depth. They are normally pinned to a pelmet board in the same way as a pelmet, through pocketed webbing tape, hand stitched to the back. They can be basted more easily directly along the front edge of the board with steel tacks, provided the tacks are covered with braid, but then it cannot be removed.

To make a pattern for a swag, cut a width(s) of mull to equal the length of the front of the board, by approximately twice the proposed finished depth. Join the widths if necessary, to form a rectangle. For a fuller swag, add approximately 4 in. (10 cm.) to either side of the bottom edge of the rectangle, then cut a diagonal line between each bottom corner and the top corners of the swag. The steeper the diagonal line the tighter the folds will be in the swag (fig. 45). Using drawing pins, attach the top edge to the pelmet board. Fold each side of the rectangle into four or five pleats, and pin them side by

side along the top edge of the board so that each pleat falls into a soft fold across the swag, forming a gentle curve (fig. 46).

The tails should fold round the returns at the corners of the pelmet board and should extend round the front to at least cover the pinned pleats of the swag. Cut a shape as suggested in fig. 47, bearing in mind the points

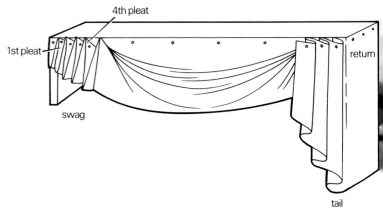

46 *Fabric pattern of swag and tail pinned to pelmet board*

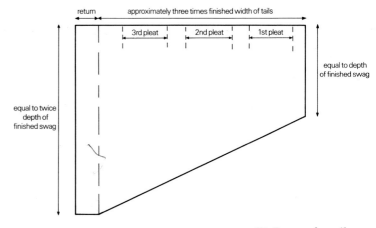

45 *Pattern for a swag*

47 *Pattern for tails*

mentioned above concerning their size. The diagonal line forms the jabot effect. Experiment to get the right proportions and then pin the top edge of the tails into the required number of pleats (two or three), leaving the returns flat. Pin the top of the pleats to the pelmet board over the ends of the swag (fig. 46). Check the whole effect and adapt as necessary.

Remove the pattern from the pelmet board, carefully keeping the pleats folded in order to mark their position with chalk or basting thread before removing the pins.

MAKING UP

Cut out the fabric and lining using the pattern pieces with a ½ in. (1.5 cm.) seam allowance all round. If you need to join widths of fabric for the swag, do so either side of a central panel, as with a pelmet (page 50) and match any patterns. Remember to cut a left- and a right-hand tail. Mark the positions of the pleats with basting stitches.

Swag

With right sides facing, pin and baste the swag to the lining on the stitching line, 1.5 cm (½ in) in from the raw edge, leaving an opening along the top edge to turn it through. Stitch, then trim the seam. Turn right side out and press. Drawstitch to close opening. Stitch braid or fringing to the right side on the lower edge. Fold the sides into the pleats and bring them to lay side by side along the top edge of the swag, pinning and handstitching them securely in position, as previously planned. Stitch braid to the top edge of the swag between the pleats.

Handstitch a length of webbing to the top edge of the lining as for Pelmets (page 50) and pin the swag to the board in the same way.

Tails

With right sides facing, pin and baste the tails to the lining, on the stitching line, leaving an opening to turn through. Machine, then turn right sides out. Press. Drawstitch the opening. Pin the pleats as previously planned and hand stitch securely in position, close to top edge. Stitch braid to the outline of the pleats, covering stitching along top edge. Attach webbing tape to the top edge of tails on the lining side, in the same way as for the swag. Pin them over the pleated ends of the swag, through the pocketed webbing tape on the back.

17   ARCHED WINDOWS

These windows are very elegant and it is well worth taking the trouble to highlight them by shaping the top of the curtains to fit the curve. Curtains for arched windows cannot be fitted onto a conventional track, nor can they be operational in the sense that they can be drawn. The heading must be in a fixed position and fitted to a thin batten which is bent and fixed to the ceiling of the curve. Screw-eyes can be fitted into the front of the batten, equally spaced apart, from which the curtain can be suspended. The curtains can then be draped back and held with tie backs, to form a beautiful outline to the window. The simplest heading to use with this style is a gathered frill as any deep, stiffened pleated heading would be difficult to position around the curve satisfactorily.

TO MAKE A PAIR OF LINED CURTAINS WITH A SHALLOW CURVED TOP

To measure your window, treat it as two sections: the curved area and the rectangular section below it.

Measure and note the lengths at positions halfway (AE) and a quarter of the way across the window (FH) plus the outer edge (CI), as shown in fig. 48, and add the depth of heading. For very wide windows, take further length measurements in between these. The more measurements you take, the more accurately you can plot the curve (fig. 49). Take width measurement CD.

To estimate your fabric and lining requirements, use the width of the rectangle (CD), instead of a track length, to calculate the fabric width, allowing double fullness. Treat the centre of the window AE as your length measurement (including depth of heading) and

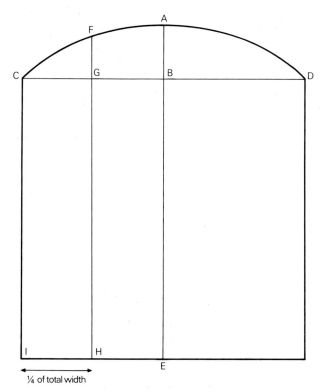

48 *Measuring an arched window*

calculate as normal (page 29) adding hem and heading allowances. You will need to cut all fabric drops to the total length measurement as at the centre of the window. For your heading-tape quantity, you will need to plot the curve as below and double the measurement.

Cut and join the widths of fabric, as for Lined Curtains (page 41), then shape the top of the two curtains in one operation as follows:

Lay the two curtains out flat on top of each other with right sides facing, and bear in mind that one curtain as laid out represents half the window (fig. 49). Mark the hemline with chalk and take one side as the centre leading edge (AE), then measure up along AE from hemline to mark the finished length. Next, mark the finished length from hemline, taken at a quarter of the way across the window (FH), at a position halfway across the fabric. Then mark finished length on the outer edge of the fabric (CI). Continue to mark further finished length measurements across the fabric, if extra measurements were taken, to correspond with the same point across the window.

Draw a line with chalk to connect these points to form the top curve. Add heading allowance by drawing a line parallel to the curve 4 cm (1½ in) away. Cut out on this line through double thickness of fabric. Make up as for Lined Curtains but with a standard gathered heading, as follows:

Heading: Turn 4 cm (1½ in) heading allowance to the wrong side and tack down. The inner edge of the turning will be slightly larger than the curtain it rests against, so it will be necessary to make tucks periodically along the edge so that the turning will lie flat. Add standard tape as in Unlined Curtains. Pull up heading to fit the curve.

For a deep, steep curve it is probably easier and more accurate to take a pattern of half the arch, and spread this to fit the curtain fabric width, as follows:

TO MAKE A PAIR OF LINED CURTAINS WITH DEEP ARCH

To make a pattern, mask half of the arch with paper and draw round the outline. Remove the pattern and trim round the outline. Then take an additional length measurement along BE.

Calculate fabric requirements, cut out and join widths as for curtains with shallow curved top, and lay curtains out flat in the same manner. Take one side as the centre leading edge. Mark the hemline with chalk, then measure up and mark off length BE on the leading edge and across the fabric width, to form line CB.

It is now necessary to spread your half pattern to fit the width of the curtain fabric as shown in fig. 50b. Cut the pattern from the curved edge to bottom edge at regular intervals (fig. 50a) and place the bottom edge of each strip on the marked line (CB). Spread and space each strip at an equal distance apart, lining up edge AB with the centre leading edge of the curtains. The wider the window the more slashes you should make. Join the highest point of each strip with a chalk line to form a curve. Remove the pattern and add a heading allowance, then continue as for the previous curtains with a shallow curve.

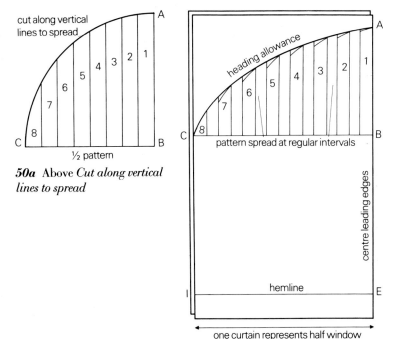

50a Above *Cut along vertical lines to spread*

50b Above right *Cutting out using a pattern for a deep curve, on a double layer of fabric*

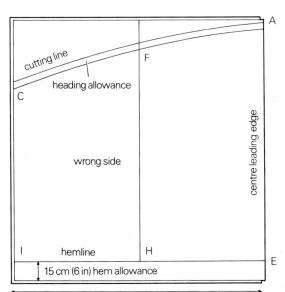

49 *Cutting out and plotting curve on double layer of fabric*

18   TIE BANDS

Tie bands hold curtains away from a window or door, allowing the fabric to fall in an attractive drape, while at the same time letting as much light as possible into a room. There are many different styles—stiff, shaped bands blend well with a traditional, formal setting and give a very professional finish. Bows can be tied in satin ribbon or in matching or contrasting fabric. Cords with tassels are available in a good range of colours and thickness and suit heavyweight curtains. Tie bands need to be attached to a tie-back hook.

To establish the size of the tie band, loop a tape measure round the drawn-back curtains; adjust it until the fabric drapes attractively, and note the length of the loop. For bows, add a minimum of 1.50 m (59 in) to this measurement to tie a reasonable sized bow.

STIFF, SHAPED TIE BANDS

It is best to make a paper pattern of your shaped band. Use the half pattern below and enlarge it on dressmaker's graph paper. You will need graph paper to the proposed length of the band. Fold it in half and use the folded edge as the centre of the band. Draw your shape, using the guide and adapting it as necessary to suit your shape and length. Cut round the outline through the double thickness of paper and open out.

For a pair of tie bands you will need approximately 40 cm (16 in) of outer fabric and lining, (use the wastage between pattern repeats for both outer fabric and lining where possible); pelmet buckram 45 cm (18 in) wide to the length of the band; approximately 30 cm (12 in) bump to soften the buckram; two tie-back hooks and two small rings.

Iron the pattern temporarily on to dampened buckram and cut round the outline. Cut out the bump to the exact size of buckram. Cut outer fabric and lining out

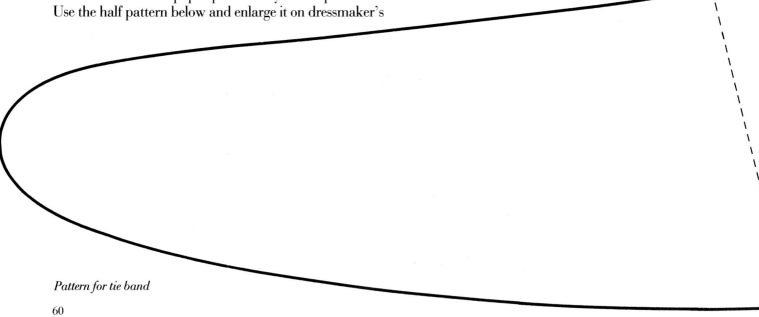

Pattern for tie band

with a 1.5 cm (½ in) seam allowance. Lay bump on one side of the dampened buckram and press to bond the layers together. Lay out the outer fabric flat with the wrong side up and lay buckram on top with the bump sandwiched in between. Dampen the edge of the buckram, bring over the seam allowance of the band and press it on to the dampened edge, notching out excess fabric on inward curves.

Press seam allowance to the wrong side on the lining and notch out in the same way. Pin the lining to the wrong side of the band and slipstitch in place. Sew a ring at either end, on lining side.

FABRIC BOW

Cut strips of fabric to the length measurement described earlier by double the finished width, plus 1 cm (⅜ in) for seam allowances. Join the strips with a plain seam and fold in half lengthways with right sides facing. Machine long edges together with a 5 mm (¼ in) seam allowance, leaving an opening for turning through and stitching diagonal ends. Turn right side out and press. Drawstitch to close opening. Sew a ring in the centre of the band to slip on to a cup hook.

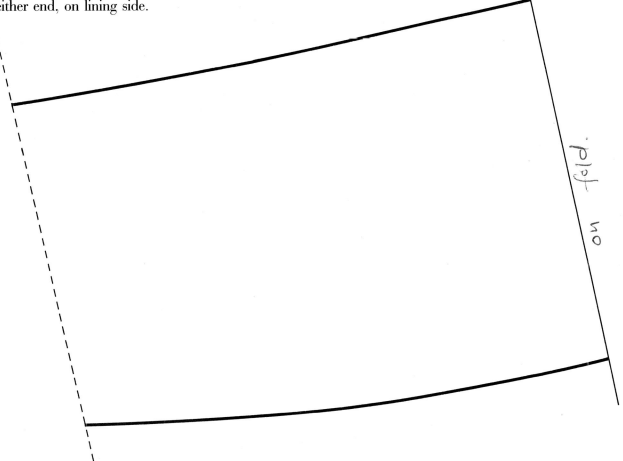

fold on

PART III

19 ROLLER BLINDS

These blinds not only offer a practical window treatment for kitchens and bathrooms, but can also look attractive in a sitting-room or bedroom when combined with curtains and made up in co-ordinated or matching fabric. Shaped hemlines are just one way to add a decorative touch. Plain fabrics can be decorated, for instance, with appliqué, or rows of contrasting ribbon. Certain fabrics will take a hand-painted design, using acrylic fabric paints. It is always advisable, however, to test your decorative technique on the fabric.

Ready stiffened and spongeable fabrics especially made for roller blinds can be bought by the metre, and have the additional advantage of being available in widths up to 175 cm (69 in), making joins unnecessary except on the widest of windows. Other fabrics should be closely woven, firm and colourfast, and must be stiffened either with an aerosol spray applied to both sides of the fabric, or by dipping into a liquid stiffening solution. It is advisable to stiffen the fabric before cutting to shape when using the latter method to allow for any possible shrinkage. Thick, textured fabrics are unsuitable as they do not take the stiffening well and also produce too much bulk around the roller. Seams are unsatisfactory on a blind as they too will cause an unattractive bulge on the roller. Where a join is necessary, it is better to glue overlapped edges together with a narrow 1 cm (⅜ in)

overlap. Alternatively, there is one kit on the market which includes narrow double-sided tape for this purpose. In many ways, however, it would be far more satisfactory to make two smaller blinds to hang side by side.

A roller blind is the simplest type of blind to make and there are several types of kit available to aid the task. All kits have accompanying instructions which should be followed carefully.

MEASURING AND ESTIMATING

Measure your window before buying your kit and fabric, using a metal rule. If fitting your blind inside a window recess you will need to measure the full recess width and depth. If fixing outside the recess, you will need to add a minimum of 10 cm (4 in) to the width of the reveal to prevent light seeping through at the sides of the blind. Your length should allow for whatever overlap you require at the top and bottom of the window.

Kits are available to fit window widths up to 245 cm (8 ft) and if the size of your window falls between sizes, buy the next size up and cut it to size according to the manufacturer's instructions.

You will need fabric fractionally wider than the measured width, by the measured length plus a minimum of 20 cm (8 in) to allow enough fabric to cover

The use of several smaller blinds at a large window, or in a bay, provides freedom to adjust the natural lighting, and creates visual interest.

the roller when pulled down, and to form a channel for a lath. For a blind with a shaped hemline, a further allowance should be added for facing the shaped edge; allow a depth of between 8 and 15 cm (3–6 in) for this depending on the depth of the edging below the lath.

TO MAKE A ROLLER BLIND WITH STRAIGHT HEMLINE

Accuracy in measuring and cutting out is essential. Mount the supporting brackets first, according to the manufacturer's instructions. Then measure the exact distance between the slot on one bracket and the round hole on the other. Cut the roller to this measurement less 3 mm (⅛ in) to allow for the end cap. Fix the end cap with the round pin over the cut end.

If using liquid stiffening solution, first stiffen the fabric, having ironed out any creases. The fabric must be cut with right-angled corners. Measure and mark the fabric to the length of the measurements taken, plus allowances for covering roller and lath. Mark the width of the blind 1.2 cm (⅜ in) less than the cut roller length with two parallel chalk lines, remembering that these lines must be square to the top and bottom marked edges. Centre any pattern. If your fabric is likely to fray, it is advisable to machine a row of zig-zag stitches inside the marked side lines and up against them. Cut out the blind with sharp scissors on the marked lines and/or against the zig-zag stitching.

Hemline

Lay the blind out flat with wrong side uppermost and form the lath channel by turning 1 cm (⅜ in) up to the wrong side along the bottom edge, then turn up a further 4 cm (1½ in). Machine in place. If your fabric is very stiff, make one 4 cm turning and zig-zag stitch over the raw edge or glue in place. Apply any trimming with glue.

Finishing off

Stitch on any surface decoration before spraying the blind. Finally apply any braid trim with glue.

To finish off all blinds, attach the blind fabric to the roller according to the manufacturer's instructions. Insert pulling cord through the cord holder and screw it to the centre of the lath on the wrong side. Insert roller into supporting brackets and adjust the tension according to the manufacturer's instructions.

20 ROMAN BLINDS

A Roman blind offers a smart, clean-cut finish to a window, with its pleats forming a soft layered pelmet when the blind is raised. These blinds are not suitable for very shallow windows as there would be insufficient depth of fabric to form into pleats. On wider windows, two smaller blinds side by side may be better.

There are two methods of making these blinds; Method 1 gives a professional finish using narrow wooden laths, which are slotted into channels in the lining to keep the pleats defined and neatly layered; Method 2 is simpler, using vertical rows of tape and rings, and creates a softer, less rigid line which is more suitable for use at a small window.

The blinds can be fitted on to a wooden batten with touch-and-close fastener for easy removal, and are operated by pulling up cords which pass through rings on the back of the blind, then through screw-eyes on the underside of the batten.

They are easy and inexpensive to make as they require only enough outer fabric to cover the actual window opening, or your desired size, plus a little extra lining when making up as Method 1. It is essential to use closely woven, firm fabric of good quality which is on grain. It is also important to measure and cut fabric accurately to ensure that the pleats not only lie squarely on top of each other when the blind is pulled up but also to ensure that the blind hangs squarely when down. Problems occur particularly when the fabric is printed off grain and the pleats follow a horizontal design on the fabric. This could result in the blind and pleats falling at an angle to the window.

METHOD 1

Measuring and estimating materials

For fitting inside a reveal, measure the window width and length. If fitting outside, extend the blind width by at least 5 cm (2 in) either side, and add to the length measurement sufficient for whatever overlap you require at top and bottom of the window.

Planning

To calculate the number and size of the pleats, the blind length is divided horizontally into sections which form the pleats. These sections should be twice the depth of a bottom pelmet, on top of which all the pleats lie. The depth of the bottom section is also approximately equal to the depth of the 'pelmet' which forms from the layered pleats when the blind is raised. To ensure that all the pleats lie at one level when the blind is raised, the top pleat section should be slightly deeper than those below it in order to cover the front of the batten and to allow for the depth of lath and rings which accumulate at the top of the blind when it is raised. Add approximately 8 cm (3⅛ in) to the top pleat section for this purpose.

Example: Overall length 132 cm (52 in)—Bottom pelmet 14 cm (5½ in); three pleat sections of 28 cm (11 in); top pleat 34 cm (13½ in). Bear in mind that all sections must add up to the overall length measurement.

Materials

Outer fabric to the measurements taken plus 3 cm (1¼ in) for top and bottom turnings (plus a further 7.5 cm (3 in) to enable the top of the blind to lie over the heading batten if fitting outside the window reveal). To the width measurement add 6 cm (2⅜ in) for side turnings.

Lining To the finished width measurement by length measurement plus an extra 7 cm (2¾ in) for each lath channel positioned at the base of each pleat (exclude channel at the base of the blind); plus 3 cm (1¼ in) for top and bottom turnings.

A *softwood batten* 50 mm × 25 mm (2 in × 1 in) to the finished width, plus angle brackets to fix it in position, and three large screw-eyes.

Laths: 25 mm × 5 mm (1 in × ¼ in) by the width of the blind less 20 mm (¾ in); you will need one for the base of the blind and one for each channel.

Plastic rings: allow two for each channel except the bottom one.

Nylon cord: To calculate the amount, add together the width of the blind plus four times the length.

Touch-and-close fastener to the width of the finished blind, plus a cleat to hold the cord.

Matching *thread*.

Making up

Cut the blind fabric with side, top and bottom turnings. Turn 3 cm (1¼ in) to the wrong side on each side edge and herringbone stitch in place.

Lining

Having decided on the number of pleats required, cut the lining as mentioned under *Materials*, above. Pin 1 cm

($\frac{3}{8}$ in) to the wrong side along the sides and machine in place. On the right side, mark the stitching lines of the channels with a faint chalk-line (fig. 51). To form the channels above bottom pelmet, bring the pairs of stitching lines together and pin with the wrong sides facing; this will form the channels on the right side of the lining (fig. 52). Tack, then machine along these lines.

Attaching lining to blind

Join the lining to the blind at hemline by placing it centrally over the blind fabric with right sides facing and bottom raw edges level. Pin, tack, then machine along

the seamline. 1.5 cm ($\frac{5}{8}$ in) in from raw edge. Trim seam allowance to 5 mm ($\frac{1}{4}$ in). Turn right side out and press the hemline.

Lay the blind out flat with lining uppermost. Make sure the lining is lying perfectly flat and smooth against blind fabric and square to it. Then pin the lining to the outer fabric across the full width of the blind, starting 3.5 cm ($1\frac{3}{8}$ in) up from the bottom edge to form the lower channel at the base of the blind. Then pin the lining to the blind as close as possible to each stitching line forming the channels, across the full blind width. Tack, then machine in place, ensuring that the stitching lines are perfectly horizontal and parallel to each other, and make sure you have not caught any of the channel fabric in the stitching. Pin the sides of the lining to the blind, excluding the ends of the channels, then slipstitch (fig. 53).

Finishing off

Turn 1.5 cm ($\frac{5}{8}$ in) of blind fabric and lining to the wrong side along the top edge. Pin, tack then machine

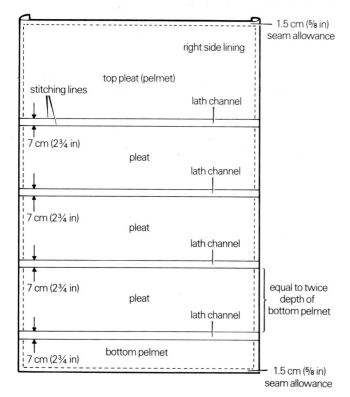

51 Roman blind—method 1; Marking lining with pleat and channel sections

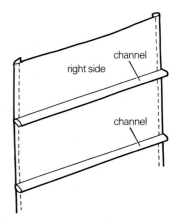

52 Forming channels in lining

the soft side of touch-and-close fastener over the raw edges.

Insert a lath into each channel, then slipstitch the ends together. Stitch two rings to each channel, except the bottom one, approximately 10 cm (4 in) in from the sides.

To cord the blind, cut one length of cord approximately twice the length of the blind, and another to the same length plus the blind width. Decide from which side you wish to operate the blind. Tie a length of cord to each of the lowest rings, placing the shortest length nearest the operational side.

Optional: Neatly cover the batten by wrapping fabric round, folding in the ends and holding in place with steel tacks.

Attach the remaining side of touch-and-close fastener to the front edge of the batten with steel tacks or along the top back edge of batten if fitting outside a reveal. Screw two screw-eyes to the underside of the batten to correspond with the two rows of vertical rings, and a third one close to the end of the batten on the operational side.

Fix the batten in place with angle brackets, then attach the blind with touch-and-close fastener. Thread cord up through rings and corresponding screw-eyes and out to the operational side. Tie cords together close to the outer screw-eye.

Screw cleat in position at the side of the window and pull up the blind. Wind the excess cord round the cleat to hold in open position (fig. 54).

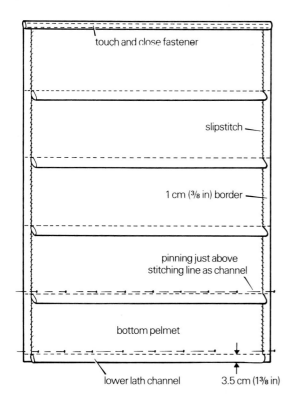

touch and close fastener

slipstitch

1 cm (³⁄₈ in) border

pinning just above stitching line as channel

bottom pelmet

lower lath channel   3.5 cm (1³⁄₈ in)

53 *Attaching lining to blind by pinning across blind in same position as channels*

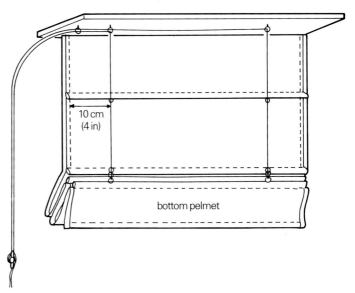

10 cm (4 in)

bottom pelmet

54 *Blind fixed to batten and cords threaded to operational side*

METHOD 2

This version has vertical rows of tapes spaced evenly across the back of the blind. Rings are attached along these tapes to form horizontal rows of rings. The pleats are formed by pulling on cords which are attached to the lower row of rings at the lath position above the bottom pelmet, and which pass up through the rings. The distance between the horizontal rows of rings should be twice the depth of the bottom pelmet to make a pleat the same size as the pelmet. On small windows, using fine fabric, as little as 10 cm (4 in) could be allocated to make a 5 cm (2 in) pleat and pelmet, but on larger windows allow between 15 and 20 cm (6 and 8 in) for a 7.5 cm (3 in) and 10 cm (4 in) pleat respectively. Measure and plan as Method 1.

NB Straight seam tape can be used instead of pocketed tape, but you will then need to sew on rings individually.

Materials

Blind *fabric* and *lining* to the width and length measurements, plus an additional 3 cm (1¼ in) on width and length for turnings.

Narrow *pocketed tape* to make vertical rows approximately 30 cm (12 in) apart (gathering tape is suitable but ignore the draw cords).

Split rings enough to position along each vertical row of tape, and spaced according to the size of the finished pleat (e.g., every 20 cm (8 in) for a 10 cm (4 in) pleat).

Nylon cord to equal the length of each vertical row of tape plus enough to thread across the top of the blind and out to one side, and then down one side.

Touch-and-close fastener to the width of the finished blind.

A *softwood batten* as Method 1, plus a screw-eye for every vertical row of tape. One *lath*, as Method 1. One *cleat*. Matching *thread*.

Making up

Cut the fabric and lining to the measurements plus turnings. With right sides facing, pin and tack the lining to the outer fabric on the seamline, 1.5 cm (⅝ in) in from the raw edge, along the side and bottom edge. Trim seams and cut diagonally across corners. Turn right side out and press.

Lay blind out flat with lining uppermost, and mark the position of the lath channel by measuring up from the hemline to a distance equal to the depth of the bottom pelmet. Draw a second line parallel to the first, 3 cm (1¼ in) away. Tack, then machine the lining to the outer fabric along these marked lines to form lath channel. Unpick stitching along one side between channel stitching to insert lath at a later stage.

At the top of the blind, turn 1.5 cm (⅝ in) to the wrong side and pin and tack the soft side of the touch-and-close fastener over the raw edge. Machine.

Mark the vertical lines for the tapes across the width of the blind at equal distances apart, approximately every 30 cm (12 in), the first and last rows starting and ending 1.5 cm (½ in) in from the sides of the blind. Cut the appropriate number of lengths of tape to the length measurement of the blind from the lath channel. Pin, and tack the tape over the marked lines, turning cut edge under at the top and bottom. Machine along both edges of the tape through the lining and the outer fabric.

Insert split rings along each tape, spacing them at an equal distance spart, at a distance to equal twice the depth of the bottom pelmet starting at lath channel. They should also align horizontally across the blind (fig. 55).

Insert the lath into the channel and slipstitch the end.

Decide from which side you wish to operate the blind. Cut a length of cord for each vertical tape, twice its length plus the distance from tape to the operational side of the blind. Tie a cord to each bottom ring and thread it up through the rings on each tape.

The clean lines of these Roman blinds fit in well with the sharp, uncluttered décor and furnishing.

Cover the batten and attach the opposite side of touch-and-close fastener, as Method 1. Insert screw-eyes to the underside of the batten to correspond with each row of tape.

Attach the blind to the batten and thread each cord through its corresponding screw-eye, then out to the operational side, passing through each screw-eye it passes. Tie the cords together and fix cleat in position.

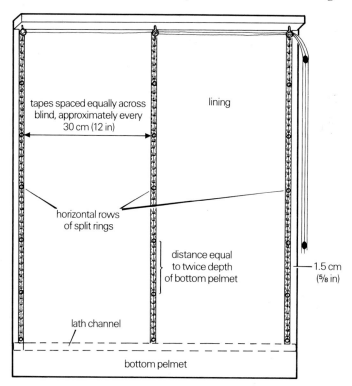

tapes spaced equally across blind, approximately every 30 cm (12 in)

lining

horizontal rows of split rings

distance equal to twice depth of bottom pelmet

1.5 cm (⁵⁄₈ in)

lath channel

bottom pelmet

55 Roman blind—method 2

21 FESTOON BLINDS

These pretty blinds give a soft, flamboyant appearance and form a scalloped hemline when drawn up. Frills can be added to the hemline and sides to further enhance their feminine appeal. Made up in lightweight fabrics, either soft or crisp, each will offer a pleasing but different effect. The former will allow the scallops to drape in folds, while the latter will create fuller, puffed scallops.

The blind can be fitted inside or outside a window reveal, and is attached to a batten and operates in a similar way to Roman Blinds, Method 2, with cords threaded through vertical rows of rings on the back of the blind (fig. 55, above). They can have a gathered or

A festoon blind used inside the window reveal gives a neat, tailored look that suits the restrained style of the room.

pencil pleated heading, which gives the fullness to the blind to create the festoons. Generally, they need fullness of two to two and a quarter times the batten length (the fuller the fabric the deeper the festoons). They look like curtains when they are down but are made slightly longer than the window length to allow for the scalloped hemline to fall at sill level. They can be lined or unlined; have rings which are handsewn in position or split rings which slot into pocketed tape. The latter method will show the stitching securing the tapes on the right side.

MEASURING AND ESTIMATING MATERIALS

Measure the width of the window opening if fitting inside the reveal, or to your desired width if fitting outside. You will need a batten to this width. For the length, measure from the top of the batten position (inside or outside reveal) to the sill. Add to this measurement 6 cm (2½ in) for hem and heading allowance, and a minimum of 20 cm (8 in) which allows the scalloped hemline to form at sill level when the blind is down, by pulling up the cords fractionally.

To estimate your fabric requirements, multiply the batten length by the desired fullness, two to two and a quarter times, then calculate as for curtains (page 29), adding extra for matching any pattern. If it is necessary to round up to the next width of fabric do not automatically include the extra fullness in the blind. Adding too much fullness to the blind will make the swags heavy and droopy. Use full and half widths in the main, and use any wastage for frills and covering the batten.

TO MAKE AN UNLINED FESTOON BLIND
with pocketed tape and split rings

Planning
You will need to establish the size and number of scallops

across the blind in order to calculate the amount of tape needed. The width of an average sized scallop on a finished blind is approximately 30 cm (12 in). Bearing this in mind, divide the batten length into equal sized scallops, and add one to the number of scallops to give the number of vertical rows of tape needed; e.g., three scallops will need four rows of tape. These tapes are spaced across the total width of the fabric at an equal distance apart, bearing in mind that the distance between them will be two to two and a quarter times the finished scallop width, depending on the fullness you allowed. If possible, plan to cover any seams with a row of tape.

Example Batten length 90 cm (36 in) using double fullness (180 cm/6 ft), i.e., 1½ widths of 120 cm (48 in) wide fabric:

Makes 3 scallops each 30 cm (12 in) wide 4 rows of tape spaced 60 cm (24 in) apart (fig. 56).

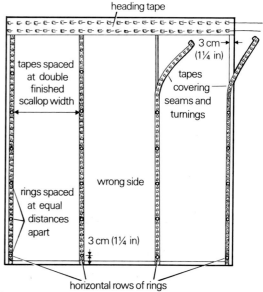

56 *Festoon blind—example: Batten length 90 cm (36 in); 1½ widths of fabric. Double fullness. Finished scallop width 30 cm (12 in)*

A festoon blind with pencil heading fitted inside the reveal gives a fresh, country look to this kitchen.

Materials

In addition to the blind fabric, as calculated above, you will need:

Pocketed *curtain tape* 1.7 cm (⅝ in) wide to equal the length of the blind for every row as calculated. Enough *split rings* to insert every 20 cm (8 in) along each row of tape. Curtain *heading tape* to total width of fabric. *Curtain hooks. Nylon cord* for each vertical row of tape, plus enough to thread across the top of the blind to one side and down side of blind. Matching *thread. Softwood batten* and *angle brackets* as for Roman Blind. Large *screw-eyes* for every vertical row of tape *Cleat. Staples* or small *screw-eyes* to space approximately every 6 cm (2½ in) along the front of the batten.

Making up

Cut the required number of widths of fabric and join them, matching any pattern, with a 1 cm (⅜ in) plain seam if they are to be covered by tape. Otherwise make a narrow french or mock french seam.

Turn 3 cm (1¼ in) to the wrong side along the side edges and tack in place. Make a narrow double-stitched hem (page 38) along the hemline.

Apply the heading tape of your choice (see Lined or Unlined Curtains).

Mark the position of the vertical tapes by folding the width of the blind into as many equal sections as the number of scallops and press lightly to form creaselines (fig. 57). Cut the required number of tapes to the length

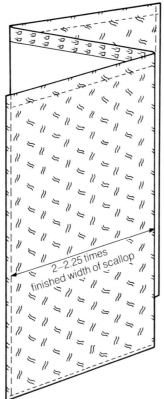

2–2.25 times finished width of scallop

57 *Blind folded into as many equal sections as the number of scallops and pressed to mark crease lines for tapes*

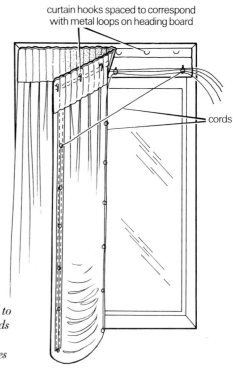

curtain hooks spaced to correspond with metal loops on heading board

cords

58 *Festoon blind fixed to heading board and cords threaded up through corresponding screw-eyes on underside of board*

of the blind fabric. Pin and tack them over the creaseline on the wrong side. Position the outer tapes over the raw edges of side turnings. Turn under the cut ends of tape at the top and bottom. Machine the tape along both edges.

Insert split rings along each tape at equal distances apart, approximately every 20 cm (8 in), starting 5 cm (2 in) up from the hem, and finishing about 15 cm (6 in) from the heading tape. Make sure the rings align horizontally across the blind.

Draw up the heading tape to fit the batten. Scallops should now be of equal size and measure their planned finished width. Insert the curtain hooks into heading tape every 6 cm (2½ in).

Neatly cover the batten as for a Roman Blind. Attach large screw-eyes to the underside to correspond with the rows of tape. Hammer large staples halfway in to form loops, or attach screw-eyes along the front edge of the batten spaced every 6 cm (2½ in).

Decide from which side you wish to operate the blind, then cut and attach lengths of cord as for Roman Blind, Method 2. Attach the blind to the batten by inserting a curtain hook into each loop of staple, or screw-eye (fig. 58). Thread the cords through the screw-eyes on the underside of the batten as for Roman Blind, Method 2 (fig. 55). Fix cleat in position, then pull cord to raise the blind, winding the excess round the cleat.

22   RUCHED BLINDS

A ruched blind with its ruffled, scalloped surface, may give the impression of using an excessive amount of fabric, but in fact it can take about the same as a festoon blind, as very little fullness is needed across its width. The effect is achieved by gathering additional fabric along the length of the blind. The amount of extra length can vary enormously to suit the type of fabric chosen and the desired finished effect. The finer the fabric used, the more length should be allowed. Soft lightweight fabrics which gather well are most suitable. Thick fabrics, particularly when used in conjunction with too much fullness, will create heavy swags which are liable to droop. These blinds are normally unlined and are often made up in sheer fabrics which are left down permanently.

Additional surface decoration is unnecessary other than, perhaps, a frill on the hemline to echo the side frill which automatically forms when the blind is gathered up along the tapes.

They are made and operated in a similar way to festoon blinds but often using more closely spaced vertical rows of gathering tape, and when drawn up the blind has an even fuller effect. No heading tape is necessary and the blinds are attached to a heading batten with touch-and-close fastener. By using narrow curtain tape to gather up the blind length (as opposed to permanent gathering stitches) the fullness can be released for cleaning. A covered lath is fitted across the back of the blind just above the scalloped hemline to keep the blind in shape (except with sheers).

TO MAKE A RUCHED BLIND WITH FRILLED HEMLINE
Measure the window width and length as for Festoon Blinds.

Width Multiply the batten length by one and a quarter to one and a half times fullness and add 6 cm (2½ in) for side turnings. Divide the result by the width of your chosen fabric to give the number of fabric widths. If it is necessary to round up to the next full width, do not automatically include all the extra fabric width in the blind as this will make the scallops deep and heavy. Use any wastage from the width for a frill and/or covering the batten and lath. Bear in mind that it is possible to make this type of blind without any fullness in the width, but with the resulting effect of tight rows of ruching and only a slight scallop on the hemline. Only use the maximum fullness when using the minimum extra length.

Length You will need to multiply the *measured length* by between one and a half to three times, depending on the weight of your fabric, to give your *cutting length*.

Fabric Requirements To calculate your blind fabric requirements, multiply the number of widths by the *cutting length*. Allow extra for matching a pattern. If there is no wastage on the width of fabric, you will also need extra for a frill and for covering a batten and lath. For a double-sided frill, you will need enough strips of fabric to equal twice the width of the blind fabric by twice the desired depth of frill, plus 4 cm (1½ in) for seam allowances.

Scallops The width of a finished scallop can be between 25–30 cm (10–12 in), depending on your fabric. Bearing this in mind, calculate the size and number of scallops, and rows of tape needed, as for Festoon Blinds. The tapes are spaced across the fabric in the same way, i.e., an equal distance apart, but spaced, in this instance, so that the distance between them will be one and a quarter to one and a half times the finished scallop width. Plan to cover any seams where this is possible.

To calculate the amount of gathering tape (1.7 cm ⅝ in wide) needed, multiply the number of rows of tape by the fabric cutting length and add 6 cm (2½ in) for each row for finishing off the tape.

Additional materials

In addition to the blind fabric and tape, you will need:

Enough *split rings* to insert along each tape at approximately 20–25 cm (8–10 in) intervals, after the blind has been gathered up to its finished length. The distance between the rings will vary according to the thickness and fullness of the fabric chosen, but they must be spaced at regular intervals. *Touch-and-close fastener* to the length of the batten. Matching *thread; nylon cord, softwood batten, angle brackets* and large *screw-eyes* as for Festoon Blinds. One *lath* as for Roman Blind. *Cleat.*

Making up

Cut out the required number of widths of fabric to the length calculated, and join them as for Festoon Blind.

Turn 3 cm (1¼ in) to the wrong side along the sides and tack down.

Divide the hem line into four equal sections and mark with a pin.

Making the double-sided frill

Cut strips of fabric as calculated and join the strips with right sides together to form one long strip using a plain seam. Press seam open. Fold and press the strip in half lengthways with wrong sides facing.

Divide the frill into four and mark these sections. Machine one row of stitching on the seamline of the frill, 2 cm (¾ in) in from the raw edge, using long stitches and loose tension. Break the thread periodically to make small sections which will ease gathering up later.

Machine a second row of stitching 5 mm (¼ in) away from the first within the seam allowance, breaking the thread at the same position as on the first row (fig. 59). Pull the bobbin threads so that each quarter section of the frill equals a quarter section of the width of the hem.

Pin the prepared frill to the hem line with right sides facing and raw edges level, matching up the quarter

Ruched blinds have a full, pretty appearance.

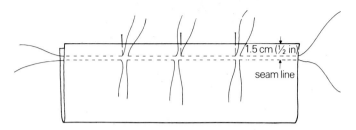

59 Machine gathering

sections. Distribute the gathers evenly and tack, then machine frill in place on seamline 2 cm (¾ in) in from raw edge. Finish off seam allowance with a self-bound finish.

Trim seam allowance of gathered frill only to a scant 5 mm (¼ in) (fig. 60a). Then turn in 5 mm (¼ in) on the seam allowance of the blind and fold the turning over the trimmed seam allowance of frill (fig. 60b). Pin, then slipstitch the binding to the machine stitching line.

At the top of the blind, turn 2 cm (¾ in) to the wrong side and sew two rows of temporary gathering stitches within this allowance by hand or machine.

Mark the position of the vertical rows of tape as for Festoon Blind. Lay the blind out flat with wrong side uppermost. Cut the required number of tapes, to the fabric cutting length plus 6 cm (2½ in) for finishing off. At one end of each tape, remove 4 cm (1½ in) of cord and knot the ends together. Trim the tape to 1.5 cm (½ in). Position this end over the frill seam allowance on hemline, turning under the knot and cut end. Pin the vertical rows of tape over the creaselines and sides as for Festoon Blind, but at the opposite end of the tapes, remove 4 cm (1½ in) of cord, trim tape to 1.5 cm (½ in) leaving the cord free for pulling up at a later stage. Turn under the cut end, finishing the top of each tape 2 cm (¾ in) down from the top of the blind. Tack, then machine the tapes in place along both edges (fig. 61). Pull up the gathering stitches along the top of the

blind until the blind width measures the length of the batten and spread the gathers evenly so that the scallops are of equal width. Pin the soft side of touch-and-close fastener to the wrong side of the top of the blind, covering the raw edge of the top turning. Pin, then machine in place. Remove the temporary gathering stitches.

Pull up the draw cords on each vertical row of tape until each tape measures the finished blind length. Spread the gathers evenly. Tie the cords neatly at the top of each tape. Insert split rings at regular intervals starting approximately 3 cm (1¼ in) up from the bottom of the

60a Self-bound seam finish

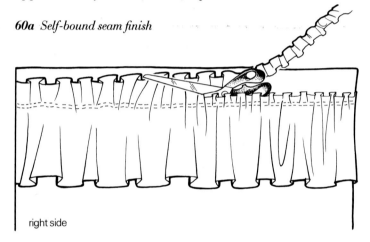

right side

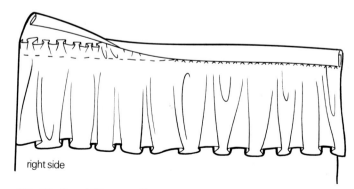

right side

60b Binding frill seam allowance

tape and spacing them between 20–25 cm (8–10 in) apart, ensuring that they align horizontally across the blind.

Cover the lath by making a casing. Cut a strip of fabric to the finished width of the blind by 10 cm (4 in) wide. Turn 1 cm (⅜ in) to the wrong side on two long edges and one short edge, then fold strip in half lengthways with wrong sides together. Topstitch sides together close to folded edges. Insert lath, then finish the casing by turning in the ends and drawstitching to close. Attach the lath with a few hand stitches to the wrong side of the blind, to the base of each tape, making sure that the width between each tape is equal and measures the finished width of the scallops as planned. This will draw the blind to the finished width at the hemline and scallops will form below the lath (fig. 62).

Attach the cords and finish off the blind as for Roman Blinds, Method 2.

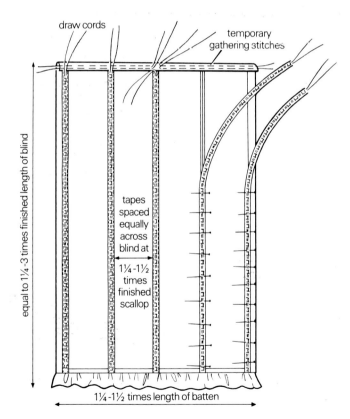

61 *Attaching tapes for gathering up the blind*

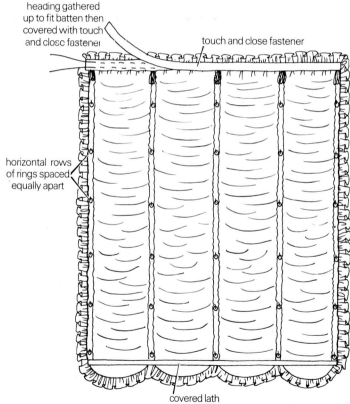

62 *Back of ruched blind with lath across bottom to keep blind in shape*

INDEX